MW01058591

# EXECUTIVE
# POWER

# EXECUTIVE POWER

Use *the* Greatest Collection
*of* Psychological Strategies *to*
Create *an* Automatic Advantage
*in* Any Business Situation

DAVID J. LIEBERMAN

**WILEY**

John Wiley & Sons, Inc.

Published by John Wiley & Sons, Inc., Hoboken, New Jersey.
Published simultaneously in Canada.

For general information on our other products and services or for technical support, please contact our Customer Care Department within the United States at (800) 762-2974, outside the United States at (317) 572-3993 or fax (317) 572-4002.

Wiley also publishes its books in a variety of electronic formats. Some content that appears in print may not be available in electronic books. For more information about Wiley products, visit our web site at www.wiley.com.

*Library of Congress Cataloging-in-Publication Data:*
Lieberman, David J.
    Executive power : use the greatest collection of psychological strategies to create an automatic advantage in any business situation / David J. Lieberman.
        p.  cm.
    Includes bibliographical references and index.
    ISBN 978-0-470-37282-1 (978-0-470-372)
        1.  Organizational behavior—Psychological aspects.   2.  Management—Psychological aspects.   3.  Personnel management—Psychological aspects.   4.  Psychology, Industrial.   I.  Title.
    HD58.7.L527   2009
    658.001'9—dc22
                                                                            2008044147

Printed in the United States of America
10  9  8  7  6  5  4  3  2  1

# Contents

# Acknowledgments

It is a genuine and great pleasure to acknowledge the creative and ultra-talented professionals at John Wiley & Sons who helped to seamlessly navigate this book's course from concept to marketplace.

The enthusiasm and zeal of the exceptionably able Vice President and Publisher Matt Holt began the process. Many thanks to my editor, Dan Ambrosio, who offered keen insights; and to Senior Editorial Assistant, Jessica Campilango, whose incandescent attitude and professionalism kept things moving along.

Now anyone who says that you can't judge a book by its cover, probably never tried to sell a book. So a big thank you to Art Director David Riedy for an outstanding book design.

Of course, books don't sell themselves. Ongoing appreciation to three extraordinary talents: Peter Knapp, Marketing Director; Kim Dayman, Senior Marketing Manager; and Jocelyn Cordova-Wagner, Associate Publicity Director, who have already begun to craft an outstanding campaign.

To those on the front lines: Immeasurable thanks to the hardworking and extraordinary sales force at Wiley for their ongoing and extraordinary efforts. And to those behind-the-scenes folks who make everything work with near-seemless perfection, a resounding thank you.

# Introduction

Most business books—whether about management, leadership, personal development, or customer service—offer nice ideas and sage insights such as *Smile and be accessible, Listen before reacting,* and *If you fail to plan, then you plan to fail.* This is good, useful advice. In today's competitive marketplace, however, businesspeople need something more potent and practical than quotes and philosophies.

For instance, you already know the importance of customer and employee loyalty. How would you like to find out the psychological strategy that *prevents* anyone from ever leaving your company? More than a few tomes offer the conventional wisdom that the customer is king, but wouldn't you really like to know the foolproof technique that will *get back* any lost client? Of course, motivating the masses is perennially necessary, but surely your ability is enhanced when you discover how to tap into your own unlimited stream of inspiration, *at will.*

*Executive Power* arms you with effective, fast-working techniques that show you, step by step, specific, carefully formulated tactics that can be applied to any situation. These are not just ideas or theories or tricks that work only sometimes and only on some people. This book offers you the opportunity to use the most important psychological tools governing human behavior, not to just level the playing field but to create an automatic advantage.

Readers get techniques that work, written in the casual, to-the-point, no-fluff, no-psychobabble style that has made David Lieberman's books so popular. They get the information *firsthand,* because it's Dr. Lieberman's techniques that the FBI uses, it's his training video that is mandatory viewing for psychological operations (psyops) graduates, he's the one who personally trains the U.S. military, he's the one who teaches tactics to senior state negotiators, he's the one who works with the foremost mental health professionals, and he's the one who trains leading business executives from more than 25 countries around the world.

There are plenty of business books that offer laws and principles and strategies and stories. Now here's one that gives specific *solutions* to real problems. From small business to big business to the professionals in between, the benefits are crystal clear. You will have the security of knowing what's really going on at all times, the power to keep potentially devastating situations from ever unfolding, and when necessary, the ability to navigate the toughest circumstances quickly and smoothly.

When the stakes are high, do more than just put the odds in your favor—fix the game so that *you can't lose.*

# A Note to Readers

Given the nearly endless multitude of variables, not all of the suggested strategies are going to be feasible for every situation. To make this book as practical as possible, a wide spectrum of tactics are offered, so that in any given situation, you will be able to apply at least one or two, and possibly more. And while each chapter is self-contained, you will find useful techniques in other chapters that will help you round out your overall approach. For the reader's convenience, these chapters are listed in the "See Also" section at the end of each chapter.

# EXECUTIVE
# POWER

# 1

## The Psychological Strategy to Gain Ironclad Loyalty: Never Lose an Employee, Customer, Client, or Patient Again

*"An ounce of loyalty is worth a pound of cleverness."*

—Elbert Hubbard (1856–1915)

What is it that makes someone stick by you, even in the darkest hour, while others run for the hills at the slightest hint that something has gone wrong?

Research shows that an unwavering sense of loyalty can, in fact, be instilled in almost anyone by applying a basic psychological strategy. Whether it's a vendor, employee, or coworker, you can make anyone more loyal—to you, your company, or your cause—faster and more easily than you may have thought possible.

You already know the basics: Communicate with your employees and customers at every opportunity, have an open-door policy and offer encouragement and praise, and have frequent face-to-face meetings, either one-on-one or as a small group. Now we'll discover how to take your skill in creating an unshakable allegiance to an entirely new level.

---

### Loyalty Is in the Cards

Jupiter Research reports that today, more than 75 percent of consumers have at least one loyalty card, and the number of consumers with two or more such cards is estimated to be one-third of the shopping population.

---

## Strategy 1: Bring Him in on the Inside

A person's loyalty is determined by which side of the fence he assumes he's on. If you bring him to your side and make him *part of your team*, he will fight your battles with you and against the other guys. To turn an outsider into an insider, you need to do two things. The first is to give him information that few people have, so he feels elite and special. The second is to give him some degree of power and authority within your organization or team.

For example, let's say that a sales manager has a salesperson whose loyalty is questionable. During a relaxed, private conversation, the manager might say something such as this: *"Chris, I want you to know that there are going to be some changes around here. The most important one is that we're close to acquiring the XYZ account. Now this is not public yet, so I need to count on your discretion."*

Once Chris agrees readily, the manager then asks him to take the reins of an aspect of the plan: *"And we think you'd be a key person on the team to figure out how we can best service them."* In this moment, Chris just became a major player on the inside, with a little bit of power, and you've just helped to create one of your strongest supporters.

You can even put your customers to work for you and thereby ensure their continued loyalty by conveying something such as: *"We're restructuring our customer service department, and we would love you to help evaluate how our inquiries are being handled. Based in part on your feedback, we'll be able to assess how effective the changes have been."*

The client will not only appreciate your valuing his input and feedback but also soon feel personally vested and connected to your company. You further solidify his loyalty by asking him to review (a task that shouldn't take more than 10 minutes) monthly customer service feedback reports.

## Strategy 2: A Part of Greatness

How people identify with their favorite sports teams is revealing. When their teams win, they say, *"We* won!" but when they lose, it's often *"They* lost!" We all want to be part of something great, to be with someone great, and to attach ourselves to a winner. To inspire loyalty, let others see the greatness *within you.*

The quickest way to lose someone's loyalty is to be perceived as dishonest or untrustworthy. Even if the person does not like what you have to say, your truthfulness speaks volumes, communicating an important message: *that you can be trusted.* Regardless of anything else, people will take their chances with someone who is principled before they will sign on with someone who tells them what they want to hear or who tries to cover up.

### A Lawyer Who Never Loses

Having never lost a single case, legendary trial attorney Gerry Spence was hired to defend a man whose alleged crime had been splashed across every newspaper in town. An overwhelming majority of townsfolk had already decided on his guilt. During jury selection, most prospective jurors insisted that while they knew of the case, they could nonetheless remain impartial. Given the skewed media attention, the seasoned attorney concluded that they were probably insincere. He decided to take his chances with a jury who felt his client was guilty and stated that they *could not be fair*. Why? Because they were honest. He had something to work with—people of integrity. The verdict: not guilty on all counts.

You can develop an ardent sense of loyalty by being known as someone who does what is right, even when an easier course of action is apparent and readily available. Therefore, always be honest in your dealings, and *never sacrifice the truth*. This illuminates fine character like a beacon in a fog of phonies.

Your integrity can illustrate itself in a variety of ways. For instance, if you are playing a game with colleagues, and a disagreement ensues over who is right, *take a position that is unfavorable to you*. Long after the game is forgotten, you will be known as the person who took the high road, even though it was not in your best interest. People will seek you out and want to be a part of what you do. By the way, since we are speaking of integrity, be sure that your position, although unfavorable to you, is genuine. You do not want to manufacture circumstances so that you can appear a certain way. Rather, where such situations arise naturally, be aware, so that you can maximize your ability to garner loyalty.

Let's take another example. If your client wants to do something that is not really in his best interest but that is advantageous to you—for example, in terms of a contract, commission, or billable hours—and you explain to him how and why it is not in his best interest (and perhaps suggest a less costly route), you will have gained a client for life.

How much greater loyalty do you feel for a mechanic or a dentist who, for example, reveals that certain work is unnecessary, even when you would never have known that on your own? A principled person stands apart in his ability to captivate unwavering loyalty.

In Robert Cialdini's classic book *Influence* (1998), he tells of a top waiter who unscrupulously used this function of human behavior to boost orders and consequently tips for larger groups of diners. Taking the initial order, the waiter would hesitate, look over his shoulder, whisper that the dish "wasn't as good tonight as it usually is," and suggest two other menu items that were slightly *less* expensive. Diners felt grateful that the waiter had done them a favor—and now perceived him as someone they could trust. The waiter received higher tips, as diners were inclined to order more expensive wines and desserts from this waiter of such seeming high integrity.

## Strategy 3: Little by Little

In a study done by Freedman and Fraser (1966), a team of psychologists called several housewives in California and asked them if they had a few minutes to answer a few questions about the household products they used. A majority agreed.

Then the researchers called again three days later but this time asked if they could send five or six men to the home to go through all of the kitchen's cupboards, pantries, and shelves as part of a *two-hour* tally of household products. The psychologists discovered that these housewives were more than *twice as likely* to agree to the *two-hour* request than a group of housewives who were asked *only* to complete the larger task. You see, if their unconscious was not first primed, the housewives had no foundation to submit to such an inconvenience. How does this work?

When we take that initial small step in one direction, we are motivated to maintain a sense of consistency to greater requests and additional investment along those same lines. The implication for imbuing others with loyalty is far-reaching.

Let's say, for example, that you want a customer to be more loyal to your organization. Invite him to the company picnic, have him speak with and get to know your employees, and ask him for references and referrals and suggestions on how you can improve your business relationship.

These small steps build internal momentum. Clearly, he *must* care about your company because he has invested himself in it. To leave you, he would need to justify to himself why he put so much time and energy into improving the relationship. This necessity forces him subconsciously to come up with reasons for staying with you, even when more favorable conditions might be found elsewhere. This is why successful salespeople—selling carpet to cars to timeshares—want to keep potential customers in their clutches for as long as possible. The more time you spend with them, the harder it is for you to justify walking away.

When people have no emotional, financial, or material investment in an enterprise, they're quicker to jump ship. Get someone involved as part of a team or a cause, little by little when things are going well, and you will find that they will stand by you in more difficult times down the road. The bottom line is this: *The more of himself he invests in you, the more he will care about you.*

This holds true for our more personal relationships as well. When a person gives, he loves the object of his giving more—and so love is planted and grows. A child receives and a parent gives; who loves more? The child cannot wait to get out of the house, while the parent is forever concerned with the child's well-being.

In fact, every positive emotion stems from giving and flows outward from us to others, whereas every negative emotion revolves around taking. For example, lust is the *opposite* of love. When we lust after someone or something, our interest is purely selfish in our desire to feel complete. When we love, however, our focus is on how we can express our love and give to the other person. It makes us feel good to give, and we do so happily. When someone we love is in pain, we feel pain. When someone after whom we lust is in pain, however, we think only about how this person's situation will affect us, in terms of our own inconvenience or discomfort.

### Little Touches Make a Big Difference

Your employees also have homes and families that are of paramount importance to them. Do not refuse them the opportunity to make personal phone calls during working hours or other basic conveniences. Be flexible when employees ask for family time off. Consider long-term and short-term rewards for your employees. The former might be profit sharing; the latter might be offering things that can make your employees' lives easier, such as a ride home when they work late, dry-cleaning services, catering services, or movie tickets and a restaurant coupon for the entire family to make up for time taken away from them when an employee must work late.

## Strategy 4: Loyalty Is Earned, Not Owed

If you want your employees to be loyal to *you*, you must be loyal to *them*. Sometimes this means supporting them when they need help to deal with customers, suppliers, or coworkers who are treating them unfairly. And sometimes it simply means being patient and understanding when they make an honest (or even not-so-honest) mistake.

Your decision to do so engages the law of reciprocation, whereby the other person feels that he owes you one. Whenever someone does us a favor, it can make us uncomfortable because it makes us feel dependent, and human beings need a sense of independence. Therefore, when we do something for someone else—that is, showing our loyalty—that person reflexively feels obligated to pay us back to make himself more emotionally solvent.

Consider an instance where a district sales manager wants to prevent a big client from considering other vendors' goods or services. Should a mistake arise on her customer's invoice, and she goes to bat for him, she will create her own insurance policy. For example, she might say, "*Mr. White, I know that the contract says 4,000 gallons of* *oil, and if you were told that you could get it at $45 a gallon, then that's good enough for me."* She then copies him on any letters that she may send on his behalf or keep him apprised of pertinent conversations or e-mails.

This single gesture will have earned her an amazing amount of credit the next time she needs him to support something important to her. If you are in a position to come to the rescue when someone else's back is against the wall, you will have earned their loyalty and gained their respect. Equally compelling, studies show that a person who had resolved to his satisfaction a serious issue *is more loyal to the company than one who never had any complaints in the first place.* This is true for dual psychological factors—the *law of reciprocation* and *emotional investment.*

---

### Keep in Mind

Research estimates that it costs five times more to gain a new customer than to keep an old one. To put it another way, if 10 percent of customers who try your product or service can be turned into lifetime loyal customers, then this can save you, on average, up to 80 percent of what it would cost, from a marketing standpoint, to gain new customers. That means, whatever the customer wants, as long as it's within the realm of reason, give it to him.

---

## Strategy 5: The Attitude of Gratitude

Imagine a parent giving each of his two children a brand new bicycle. One child is effusive in his appreciation. The other barely mumbles a thank-you, only to ask for a basket and bell 10 minutes later. Which child do you think the parent will be more eager to give to next time?

One of the prevailing yet subtle forces behind loyalty is *gratitude.* Anytime you have the opportunity to express your appreciation to another person—whether a thank-you note for some good advice, a brief e-mail, or small gift—you put yourself into a category all by yourself. Most of us complain about one thing or the other, and as soon as we get what we want, we move on and don't look back . . . until the next time we need something. Instead, take the time to express your gratitude, and in these egocentric times, you will stand out as a person of extraordinary character.

It makes us feel good to give—but not to feed a bottomless pit. Yes, showing appreciation for another person's efforts is the right thing to do, but you will also find that others are always more willing and even eager to help you out, again and again—because you made them feel good about themselves, and you have shown yourself to be worthy of their effort and support.

See also:

- Chapter 8: *Get Back Any Customer You've Lost, No Matter Why They Left*
- Chapter 18: *Master the Art of Charisma with the Complete Psychological Formula for Instant Likability.*

# 2

# Super Spin Control: Quickly Dilute the Impact of Negative Publicity

*"Some are born great, some achieve greatness, and some hire public relations officers."*
—Daniel J. Boorstin (1914–2004)

No doubt you've heard the old expression "Any publicity is good publicity." But when it comes to corporate media relations, nothing could be further from the truth. In the 21st century, the notion that all publicity is good is surely eclipsed by another old adage: "Bad news travels fast."

The proliferation of 24/7 cable news channels, coupled with the meteoric rise of the Internet, has made it possible for bad news to spread like wildfire. Newsrooms and blogs actively solicit information from citizen journalists, who create new risks. Cell phones and PDAs can transmit documents and live-at-the-scene photos to the blogosphere and newsrooms at warp speed, pressuring a company to respond immediately. All of this is fine, even optimum, *if* you are clear about what your response should be.

## The Five Tenets to Super Spin Control

The Chinese don't have a character for the word *problem;* rather, a combination of two symbols is used—opportunity and crisis. Indeed, a crisis offers a company the opportunity to not just *survive* a public relations predicament but to *thrive* because of it. Managed well, a crisis can be an opening to reinforce a company's reputation, build brand identity, and send a positive message about a product or service. Many companies have seen their fortunes improve as the media and the public applauded their crisis response.

Although your company may bear some, if not all, culpability, *the degree to which the public holds you accountable is quite malleable*—and depends largely on your *ensuing* actions. The following five tenets offer you the ability to capitalize on the opportunity to not just minimize the downside but maximize the upside.

Case in point: In 1982, cyanide was discovered in Tylenol capsules, a product used by an estimated 100 million people. The Tylenol tampering case was a media debacle of potentially catastrophic proportions for manufacturer Johnson & Johnson. But Johnson & Johnson cooperated fully with the media from the outset and announced an immediate recall of all Tylenol packages. The result? Johnson & Johnson earned high praise from the media and high marks for integrity from the public. They later introduced tamper-resistant packaging and generated more positive follow-up publicity.

## Tenet 1: Be Proactive

Act quickly and decisively. If you know your company is about to get unwanted attention, go public with the story first. (The same is true for any type of office rumors or workplace grumblings; moving in front of the story allows you to shape it and control it, as opposed to having to spend resources to deny aspects that are untrue or inconsequential.)

---

### Jumping the Gun

Move in proportion to the break itself. In other words, don't use an atomic bomb to smash an ant; this just creates fallout for no good reason. While making sure that you are in front of the news, wait just long enough to see if the story has legs. In *High Visibility* (2005), the authors point out that people usually don't start following a situation until the second time they hear it, so if there is going to be news about it, be sure that it will become news before you respond. The last thing you want to do is create momentum for your own story.

---

The biggest myth is that ignoring negative publicity sends a message that the event is a nonstory. In today's media, silence implies guilt. Much like our Fifth Amendment, jurors are suspicious of defendants who choose not to take the stand in their own defense. Even though the presumption of innocence should be preserved, it is human nature to conclude that the innocent are eager to speak out on their own behalf.

Even worse, silence is often mistaken for apathy: Your company does not care enough about the little guy to spend your precious time and resources to help the public by clarifying the circumstances and your role. So, where necessary, make your voice heard, loud and clear.

## Tenet 2: Apologize and Explain Exactly What Happened

If your company made a mistake, admit it up front—with as little legalese as possible. Focus on delivering an empathetic, sincere message instead of simply reciting careful legal language. Analysis shows that the more human the response, the more forgiving the public.

Additional research on corporate apologies looks at the question of *attribution*, suggesting the need for a clear cause for the harm associated with the individual or company. Apologizers need to explain *why* the event occurred, either by taking the blame themselves or by citing other factors, says Maurice E. Schweitzer, who, along with Wharton colleagues John Hershey and Eric Bradlow, researched and wrote the paper "Promises and Lies: Restoring Violated Trust."

Other research details that the type of *why* makes all the difference. In an intriguing 2004 study of annual reports, Fiona Lee (University of Michigan) and Larissa Tiedens (Stanford) looked at how various companies—over a 21-year period and across a range of industries—used their annual report's letter to shareholders to explain company performance and whether the *type* of explanation correlated to the company's stock price the following year.

Their findings showed that stock prices were higher—14 to 19 percent—one year later when *companies blamed poor performance on controllable factors* rather than on external issues. For the period studied—1975 through 1995—companies that took personal responsibility for a bad year realized better stock performance the following year than did firms that blamed external, uncontrollable factors, such as bad weather or the state of the economy.

This finding is counterintuitive, in part because when it comes to *personal* apologies, the psychology reverses itself. For example, if you are late to a meeting or miss an appointment, laying fault elsewhere *reduces* the extent to which the other party takes it personally. The thinking is: *It's not that he doesn't respect me enough to show up on time, it's that there was an accident and traffic was backed up for miles.*

Our ego, which looks to make everything that happens be about us—hence the word *egocentric*—is at all times engaged in interpersonal relationships but is less of a factor in the impersonal corporate arena.

To be clear, taking personal responsibility for your mistakes is proper, shows stellar integrity, and enhances others' perception of you. The degree to which circumstances are beyond your control, however, should be explained.

## Tenet 3: Give the Full Story

Chris Nelson, who leads the issues and crisis management group as vice president of Ketchum, a global public relations firm, advises companies to disclose the facts about the event as quickly as possible. If you think that by giving out information in dribs and drabs, the public will more easily digest what is happening, you are making a common, though severe, mistake. A bit of news just forces the media to dig and make it a bigger, ongoing story, because you've just guaranteed that whatever they find will be news. Conversely, if you make all of the news yourself, quickly and upfront, there is nothing left for anyone to add, and the story fizzles out faster.

Surprisingly, considerable evidence suggests that erring on the side of the *worst case scenario* works to your advantage—because then *any* further news is now good news, and *this* becomes the focus of the story. This concept is evident with earnings statements. A public company can double revenue and triple profits, but if earnings do not beat even their own forecasts, the stock is often punished because the current price already reflects expectations.

### *Air France v. Bridgestone*

History shows us that events don't damage a company; most often the company's response to events is what matters. The following example illustrates how the handling of a disaster (based on the preceding three tenets) largely determines the direction of the aftermath.

In the summer of 2000, two strong brands experienced a publicity crisis, each involving many deaths: Air France's Concorde crashed, killing all passengers onboard. Bridgestone recalled 6.5 million tires, tires that were linked to 174 deaths and hundreds of injuries.

Air France and Bridgestone established very different crisis communications initiatives. Following its tire recall, Bridgestone declined public comment. But Air France's chairman, Jean-Cyril Spinetta, was a highly visible and effective communicator after the Concorde crash. He immediately grounded all Concorde jets and traveled to the crash site. He attended the funeral services for the victims. He sent a strong, clear message about his concern for the victims' families and for the safety of future passengers.

Oxford Metrica, an independent adviser on risk, value, reputation, and governance, investigated why some companies recover from a crisis better than others. Its studies show a clear correlation between open communication policies and stock share value. One study compared the share prices of Bridgestone and Air France in the aftermath of their crises.

Bottom line? Air France's stock dropped only 5 percent during the first few days after the crash, and *then began to steadily rise.* Bridgestone's stock sank 50 percent in the first 50 days following the tire recall.

## Tenet 4: Walking the Line of Ambiguity

Speak only in vague terms when it comes to the negative, and be precise and specific about what is positive and true. A September 2007 study discussed the effects of a pamphlet issued by the Centers for Disease Control and Prevention to counteract myths about the flu vaccine:

The federal Centers for Disease Control and Prevention recently issued a flier to combat myths about the flu vaccine. It recited various commonly held views and labeled them either "true" or "false." Among those identified as false were statements such as "The side effects are worse than the flu" and "Only older people need flu vaccine."

When University of Michigan social psychologist Norbert Schwarz had volunteers read the CDC flier, however, he found that within 30 minutes, older people misremembered 28 percent of the false statements as true. Three days later, they remembered 40 percent of the myths as factual.

Younger people did better at first, but three days later they made as many errors as older people did after 30 minutes. Most troubling was that people of all ages now felt that the source of their false beliefs was the CDC. (Vedantam 2007)

When rumors (true or otherwise) are mentioned, even in the process of proving them wrong by a reputable source, people still misinterpret and misremember what is true and what is not. The public has a very short memory. Don't remind them of what they are more than willing to let go of and forget. This advice ties into our final tenet.

## Tenet 5: Move On!

You must stay focused on moving forward by getting out of crisis mode as quickly as possible. Back in the 1980s, McDonald's was faced with a rumor that its hamburger meat was made of worms. In response, McDonald's took out ads and put up posters in their restaurants saying they don't use worm meat, because it doesn't make any sense—it's more expensive than beef! This logical and reasonable response shut down the rumors, but the strategy failed to consider the focus on moving forward. Here's why the campaign went so wrong.

Commenting on research conducted after the incident, Wharton Professor Mary Frances Luce states, "McDonald's would have been better off focusing on other things." This study compared the strategy of directly refuting the rumor (as McDonald's did) to a strategy that asked consumers for their opinions on *unrelated aspects* of the McDonald's experience, such as its French fries and its restaurant playgrounds.

Even though people didn't really believe McDonald's hamburgers contained worms, they would just as soon go to a place that was not connected to the idea of worms. So by using a survey to strengthen non-worm associations (the French fries and playgrounds) rather than by immediately denying the rumor, the company would have had a more effective response.

---

### Free Publicity!

A regional video rental chain had gotten some bad press in the local papers from complaints that their DVDs were too often scratched and unviewable. The company response? *"The quality of our rentals are second to none. To prove it, we're giving five free movie rentals for all new and existing customers."* The result? The stores did a booming business, thanks to publicity that they couldn't have afforded to buy. Had they simply disputed the claim, they would have missed a golden opportunity to gain new customers.

---

See also:

- Chapter 17: *Sway The Room: From Jury Rooms to Board Rooms, How One Voice Can Change the Choir.*

# 3

## Spin Control When It's Personal: Shutting Down the Gossip and Rumor Mills

*"Whoever gossips to you will gossip about you."*

—Spanish Proverb

Gossip has always been around and always will be. The psychological motivation is threefold: (1) The misfortunes of others give us the opportunity to feel better about our own behavior; (2) if we are busy gossiping about every other person's life, we can avoid dealing with what is wrong with our own lives; and (3) gossip gives us the illusion of power and control. When others know who the gossip go-to person is, he is sought out for the latest information, making him feel important. He is undoubtedly the person who has to give hints about birthday presents and surprise parties; he beams with pride as a captivated audience hangs on his every word.

A coworker whispers a piece of juicy gossip to her office mate. A victimless crime? Hardly. Everyone pays a price. Many of us at work have been the subject of a formal campaign or a casual victim of gossip. When you try to convince people that the rumor isn't true, many people treat your response as a kind of confession that the rumor is indeed true. Naturally, then, we need a more sophisticated approach.

Here are some exceptionally effective methods of damage control that you can use to your advantage. Let's see how a little psychology can help you shut down the rumor mill and keep new ones from springing up.

## Strategy 1: Shine the Light

Because anonymity lessens inhibitions, human beings are capable of inflicting greater pain—be it emotional or physical—when our identity is hidden. As part of an experiment, psychologist Philip Zimbardo (1970) dressed New York University women in white coats and hoods. They were asked to give electric shocks to a woman. (Of course, the shocks weren't real, but the participants believed that they were.) They pressed the shock button *twice as long* as did another group of women who were not masked and were wearing clearly visible name tags.

As illuminated by the mob mentality, whereby the identity of each person is diluted in a crowd, the great philosopher Friedrich

Nietzsche once mused, "Insanity in individuals is something rare, but in groups, parties, nations, and epochs, it is the rule." In any given situation where our identity is shielded from others, our sense of right and wrong has the potential to become watered down. That's why rumors thrive in secrecy, but when you expose the source, the well dries up.

---

### I See You

In a study conducted on Halloween trick-or-treaters, children arriving at a test house were asked to take only one piece of candy. Those who were identifiable (not anonymous) and by themselves took more than one candy only 8 percent of the time. However, when the children arrived as a group, a group leader was made responsible for the entire group's behavior, and the individuals within the group were anonymous, *80 percent took more than one candy* (Diener et al. 1976).

---

Further research shows that when *we* cannot see the person both literally and figuratively (as a real person), our ability to feel empathy and compassion is equally compromised. For this reason, the psychological trauma for a pilot who drops a bomb on a city is often less than for a ground soldier who has had to shoot one man at point-blank range.

These studies and many more like them demonstrate that the best tactic to stop gossip is to go directly to the person who started the rumor and inform her that you are aware of what she is doing. In addition, make her sensitive to the fact that there is a *real person*, you, harmed by these rumors. By exposing her and humanizing yourself, you make it extremely difficult for her to continue her ways. Best of all, if you don't feel that you can do this in person, a *handwritten* note is often equally effective and in some cases more so. This is true because we tend to believe more what we read than what we hear. The person can read your note again and again, letting it sink in, and you avoid his getting defensive in a face-to-face confrontation.

# Strategy 2: Dissecting a Rumor

The previous strategy works when you know the source, but what if you don't? Or for that matter, what if you know who the gossiper is, but she doesn't seem to care?

Whether a rumor spreads like wildfire and damages your good name or it sputters out is based on two variables: if they are *interesting* and sound *believable*. As the saying goes, "A partial truth is more dangerous than a total lie." No one gossips about what is obviously false. That's not even gossip; it's storytelling.

The psychological solution, then, is instead of denying or minimizing the rumor, *embrace it, embellish it, and make it even more outrageous than it is*. The more unbelievable a rumor becomes, the less it—and others—will be taken seriously. When a story no longer makes sense, it becomes less interesting, and those who once believed it wonder who is telling the truth. When believability diminishes, so does the rumor.

In more challenging circumstances, you can take this a step further. We know that being able to deliver interesting and small morsels of the truth is what drives her, so we can use this to quash the rumors before they get started. Feed her tales of unbelievable stories, so she won't know what to believe, and when she starts to spread them around, she will become as interesting as the gossip magazines that line the shelves at the supermarket checkout. Once the gossip starts spreading these rumors, each word that comes out of her mouth damages her own reputation. (Let's keep in mind, though, that you don't want to provide rumors that cause insult or injury to a third party.)

---

### Celebrity Gossip

What happens when the rumor is a little true *and* it's already known? The absolute best method for damage control is to show *complete humility*. This completely disarms others. They no longer have a fight. What do they win? If you did something incredibly inappropriate, *do not* try to defend your behavior. Instead, respond with "I feel so foolish." This one sentence accomplishes *three* critical objectives: First, it shows that you know what you did was unacceptable—which means that you're unlikely to do it again. Second, it shows that you're human, and people actually like us more when we acknowledge something embarrassing and then take personal responsibility for it. Third, it shows complete honesty—and we are much more forgiving of an honest person. Take note of how the celebrity world works. Whenever a celebrity admits fault, and makes fun of himself—not the situation—which shows humility and recognition that what he did was wrong, the public forgives and forgets. It is when a person denies the report or takes a pompous stance that the media delight in tearing him down. One who has complete humility tears himself down, so there is nothing left for anyone else to do—except, of course, build him back up.

There will be times when you're going to want to root out the negative influence of gossiping before the rumors begin. The following strategies are for dealing with the worst of the gossipmongers.

## Strategy 3: Redefine Power

When someone feels powerful because he knows the latest and believes that he is liked because of his inside information, he is not likely to stop. He has no incentive to. If, however, he learns that people like and respect a person who can keep a secret, then the force that pulled him toward gossiping is the same force that now holds him back. The esteem he thought he was receiving is no longer there, but it can be earned if he holds his tongue.

For example, let's say that you want your coworker, Lauren, to stop coming to you with every bit of information she hears. When Lauren overhears how you admire Jennifer because she will quickly change the subject if a coworker is spoken of in an unflattering or negative light, Lauren will curtail her gossiping—it simply doesn't do anything for her anymore and, in fact, harms the way she craves to be perceived.

We gossip almost exclusively to those we are trying to impress. If we are not successful in building ourselves up through telling tales, then our impetus dissipates.

---

### The Good Life

One of the best things you can do is try to live your life in a way that makes rumors about you hard to believe. Try to remain focused in your life, and show that you are a person with good values—and that you hold tightly to those values. When you show yourself to be a good person living a moral life, the rumor mill will slow down because it won't have anything to run on.

---

## Strategy 4: Ask for Help

By coming into the situation with a complete and total sense of vulnerability, you can root out the most insidious gossiper. Let's take a look at the psychology.

A car cuts us off on the road, and we are curious to see what the driver looks like. Why? Because we want to see if this is someone who looks like he would do such a thing to us on purpose. A little old lady sitting in the driver's seat would not enrage us as much as a young male smoking a cigarette with music blaring from his car's open windows. Most of us would assume that the old woman simply didn't see our car but the young man did it to us on purpose.

We often, unconsciously, look to the situation to determine how personally we should take what is happening. Objectively speaking, our behavior is insane. We speed up, risking an accident, to catch up to the other car and see how mad we should get!

Keep in mind that the more arrogant a person appears to be on the outside, the more vulnerable and helpless he is on the inside.

Our compassion naturally emerges for children, the elderly, the sick, and even animals, because we more easily see their vulnerability via their appearance. Although we have a harder time connecting with the reckless driver because of his demeanor, we must recognize that our ego is the indicator of how well we see the reality beyond the façade.

So how does this psychology play out in the gossip situation? When you approach the gossiper with a deep sense of defenselessness, his own ego diminishes. The wall of "I am me and he is he" is broken down, and where there is no ego, there is connection. The target on your back automatically shrinks because this person, in that instant, feels your pain as his own.

Before, we spoke about humanizing yourself. Here, you needn't confront this person with what he is doing. Rather, simply, *ask for his help* to end your ongoing suffering at the hands of those who are spreading those harmful and hateful rumors.

---

### Straight Talk

If this behavior is part of a larger pattern and you have an ongoing relationship with this person, take a look at the following: At the core of interpersonal relations is that a person will treat you the way you train him to. You always have the option to call his attention to his behavior and let him know that it is not acceptable and will not be tolerated.

---

See also:

- Chapter 7: *Turn a Saboteur into Your Greatest Ally*
- Chapter 9: *Managing Difficult People: The Psychology behind Royal Pains*
- Chapter 16: *Bully-Proof Yourself and Your Office*
- Chapter 18: *Master the Art of Charisma with the Complete Psychological Formula for Instant Likability*
- Chapter 19: *The Amazing Method for Getting Along with People Who Are Emotionally Unwell*

# 4

## Turbo-Boost Morale and Keep Your Employees Productive, Motivated, and Happy . . . All without Spending a Dime

*"The best morale exists when you never hear the word mentioned. When you hear a lot of talk about it, it's usually lousy."*
—Dwight David Eisenhower (1890–1969)

Morale, in an organizational setting, is a collective state of being, the prevailing spirit of the group, as evidenced by the group's confidence, enthusiasm, discipline, and inclination to do the job as well as it can be done. Workplace morale, however, can be a slippery, and often mercurial, dynamic.

One popular belief in recent years among human resource managers is that simply being nice to your employees improves morale. It doesn't hurt, but the fact is, people spend large chunks of their lives at work, and it takes more than simple etiquette or periodic pep talks to boost spirits.

Moreover, managers tend to assume that any effective morale-boosting program will have a dollar figure attached, whether it's a financial incentive plan, salary increases, or an array of expensive benefits. Business owners often complain that people go where the money is. "False!" says consultant Roger E. Herman (2000). "All the studies show otherwise. People are hungry for opportunities to grow into their jobs. They crave advancement, both in position and stature, and in responsibility and opportunity."

Research reveals that the true satisfiers—what keeps employees happy—can't even be bought. Instead, the application of a little psychology brings more successful low-cost or no-cost opportunities to enhance morale.

## Jumping Ship

The consulting firm Employee Retention Strategies reports a startling statistic: In a 2007 survey conducted by Society of Human Resource Management (SHRM) and the *Wall Street Journal*'s CareerJournal.com, 75 percent of employees polled said they were "looking for a job."

# Strategy 1: Seek Out Input and Participation

People want to contribute to a cause they believe in that recognizes the value of their participation. Therefore, allowing employees to freely speak their minds within the organization is a key morale factor.

Consider a recent NRBI case study designed to analyze the root causes of a major health care provider's low employee morale and high turnover rate. The primary underlying psychological factor affecting employees that the National Business Research Institute (NRBI) found was that *employees did not feel that supervisors appreciated their input.*

A great ideas program was NRBI's most successful corrective strategy. Employees were asked to submit ideas on how to make the company more efficient, cut costs, or increase revenue. They were told that all ideas would be evaluated and that there would be no limit to the number of ideas selected for merit. All employees who submitted ideas that were implemented received company-wide recognition and a bonus correlated with the financial impact of the idea on the company.

The great ideas program, which increased NRBI survey scores by a blockbuster 60 percent, was successful for these reasons:

- It encouraged employee feedback and upward communication.
- It was open to everyone but rewarded only those who earned it.
- The bonuses awarded were subsidized by the additional money that the program itself generates; it pays for itself, and then some.

Invite employees to contribute to management discussions and participate in solving organization problems. Research suggests that employees are motivated by personal interaction, discussion, and the opportunity to offer and receive feedback. Therefore, create a democratic workplace (or designated times) where everyone has the opportunity to participate in making (important) decisions.

When you foster an environment that empowers employees—letting them set their own duties, deadlines, goals, and the like—they take ownership of their own corporate destiny and become more inspired.

Please do not underestimate the powerful emotional impact of bestowing employees with even a modicum of control. In unrelated research, residents of a nursing home who were given more autonomy—such as the ability to make strictly minor decisions, along the line of being able to choose meal options from a menu, instead of being served the day's fare, and having the ability to choose from several destinations for short outings—were not as prone to sickness, and the *annual death rate was cut in half* (Rodin 1994).

If the opportunity to choose between stuffed cabbage and veal chops can double the life span of an elderly person, imagine what empowering your employees can do for morale.

## Strategy 2: Socialization, Appreciation, and Recognition

An analysis of morale-boosting strategies would not be complete without a careful examination of the work of Harvard Business School professor Elton Mayo and his associates, F. J. Roethlisberger and William J. Dickson, in their groundbreaking 1927–1932 research project at Western Electric Company's Hawthorne Works plant (Mayo 2007).

Hawthorne Works employed 40,000 workers who designed, assembled, and tested switchboards, cable and wire harnesses, relays, switching systems, and other telecommunications equipment.

The Hawthorne researchers were the first to discover a group life among workers and demonstrate that interpersonal factors are critical influences on worker morale. The Hawthorne project, in fact, is often credited with launching the field of industrial psychology.

The Hawthorne experiment dispelled the myth that individual aptitudes are the most reliable predictors of job performance. Although aptitude does indicate an individual's physical and mental potential, what matters most, productivity, is strongly influenced by social factors. Workers have a strong need to cooperate and communicate with coworkers. *Isolation is demotivating.* We are social animals.

Encourage interaction between employees and find ways to promote camaraderie and a collaborative community. Social interaction positively influences employee cooperation, sparks enthusiasm about coming to work every day, and increases morale.

Alas, much more was revealed in this study. In one sense, the Hawthorne studies were an experimental design cautionary tale. The experiment was designed to measure the specific impact of motivational incentives, job satisfaction, resistance to change, group norms, worker participation, and effective leadership. However, there was no definitive correlation—either positive or negative—between productivity and independent variables such as monetary incentives or work breaks. The performance of the Hawthorne workers *continued to improve, no matter what new variables were introduced*—instead of fluctuating with each variable, as was expected. Why?

Performance improved because the workers were told that they were part of an important experiment. The researchers realized that the psychological stimulus of being singled out and made to feel important spurred increased productivity, independent of any specific condition being tested. This phenomenon has since been known as the Hawthorne Effect.

An amazingly uncomplicated yet powerful component to infusing morale in the workplace atmosphere is simply remembering to say *thank you.* Employees need recognition for their achievements, and perhaps most important, they need to be singled out from time to time. Don't forget to express appreciation to the invisible employees—the receptionist, the janitor, a file clerk.

Ferdinand Fournies, author of *Why Employees Don't Do What They're Supposed to Do* (1999), advises managers to praise employees immediately upon successful completion of a project and adds that praise should be specific and honest: "Thanks for finishing the report ahead of schedule. The conclusion was especially impressive."

Employees need to feel that they will receive equal recognition for their contribution to team projects, and each needs to feel like a valued member of the team. Even though you may think it juvenile, look for opportunities to celebrate successes publicly, especially when employees go the extra mile. Publish your appreciation in the company newsletter or post letters of appreciation on the staff bulletin board.

In *The Ten Ironies of Motivation* (2002), reward and recognition consultant Bob Nelson adds: "More than anything else, employees want to be valued for a job well done by those they hold in high esteem."

---

### Eliminate the Dead Weight

In *The Human Capital Edge* (2001), authors Bruce Pfau and Ira Kay note that failure to discipline or fire nonperformers is one of the most dangerous mistakes an organization can make. High-performing employees are troubled when nonperformers are paid the same and frequently cite this grievance in exit interviews. In fact, they want nonperformers to be fired.

---

## Strategy 3: Invest in the Manager-Employee Relationship

People leave managers and supervisors more often than they leave companies or jobs. The Hawthorne experiment demonstrated that the supervisor-employee relationship influenced the manner in which an employee carries out directives. The mere act of showing employees that you're concerned about them—*even without praise*—spurs better performance.

Morale begins with employee devotion, and devotion is bred through manager-employee relationships. According to Tom Rath, author of the best-selling *Vital Friends* (2006), employees who have a close friendship with their manager are 2.5 times more likely than others to be satisfied with their jobs.

He cites a novel 2006 Gallup-Princeton study in which participants were asked to reconstruct their day and report overall enjoyment of key moments. Then they ranked people they spent time with to create a list of people they enjoy being with. Clients and customers were third from the bottom, and coworkers ranked next to last, followed by bosses, who were dead last. Interacting with the boss was also rated, on average, as being less enjoyable than cleaning the house.

Rath says that one of the secrets of being a great manager-teacher is getting to know each employee as an individual and tailoring management to each employee's preferences. "The best managers in the world are not only experts in systems, processes, and technical competencies—they are experts in your life," Rath says. "And, because of this, they increase your engagement and productivity at work."

Employees want and need managers who care about their lives beyond the workplace. Gallup has asked more than 8 million people to respond to the statement "My supervisor, or someone at work, seems to care about me as a person" and found that people who agree with this statement are more likely to stay with the organization, have more engaged customers, and be more productive.

The Hawthorne experiment highlighted the reality that organizations that don't devote enough attention to people and cultural variables are consistently less successful than those that do. Modern research suggests that organizations that devote attention to the deep sentiments and intricate relationships connecting employees will be consistently more successful than those that don't. In other words, morale boosting is more about humanity than about mechanics or money.

## The Small Business Advantage

Morale boosting is generally less challenging in smaller companies. A recent Gallup study commissioned by the Marlin Company indicated that 41 percent of workers in small companies were "strongly satisfied" with their jobs, as compared with 28 percent of workers in large companies. In addition, 46 percent of workers at large companies say that the job often interferes with personal and family needs, as compared with 31 percent of employees at small companies. And employees at small companies are more than twice as likely to find social support at work.

# Strategy 4: Where Money Can Damage Morale and the Power of Creativity

A competitive atmosphere is often unproductive and, in fact, even damaging. Alfie Kohn's book *Punished by Rewards: The Trouble with Gold Stars, Incentive Plans, A's, Praise, and Other Bribes* (1999) includes numerous workplace studies indicating that, when employees are asked to rank what's most important in their jobs, money ranks well behind factors such as interesting work and enjoyable coworkers. Interestingly, when managers are asked what matters most to their employees, they tend to rank money at the top. They're managing their employees according to a false premise.

According to Kohn, at least 70 studies have found that rewards tend to undermine interest in the task or behavior itself. He cites the compelling case study of Marshall Industries, a large California electronic components distributor whose "myopic, pop-behaviorist sensibility" influenced the company to lean heavily on financial incentives. Then the lightbulb moment arrived: Financial rewards were actually *stunting* company growth. First, CEO Rob Rodin eliminated contests and other practices that pitted employees against each other, then he eliminated management incentives, and finally, he replaced pay-for-performance compensation, such as commissions, with a base salary.

The result? Morale soared. Salespeople cooperated with each other. Turnover—one of the most expensive hidden costs of reward systems—was reduced by 80 percent. And sales (and profitability) increased dramatically. In five years, Marshall's stock rose from $8 to $40, and annual sales moved from $575 million to $1.3 billion.

Let's spend another moment on this idea of incentives, because it lies counter to most people's understanding of what motivates a person.

In an organizational setting, the word *motivation* often connotes *reward* and *punishment*. After all, the reward-punishment paradigm has been our modus operandi since the Industrial Revolution, and only recently have we begun to question its effectiveness. Reward-punishment models—classic remnants of B. F. Skinner's behaviorism—assume that behavior is motivated solely by extrinsic factors.

Extrinsic motivation theories view the task itself as a means to an end, a prerequisite for receiving a reward or avoiding a punishment. For intrinsically motivated behaviors, by contrast, there is no apparent reward or external reinforcement; the activity itself is reward enough. Extrinsic rewards, it turns out, can actually be demotivating.

Fascinating research shows an interesting relationship between reward and behavior. In one experiment, people who were paid $100 to perform a task rated it as more difficult and stressful than did those being paid $25 to perform the same task under identical conditions. And as the size of the reward increases, their motivation and interest decline (Freedman and Fraser 1966).

What this study and others like it show is that when money (or, for that matter, any external compensation) is introduced into the equation, our minds assume that the task or job *requires* such compensation. Numerous findings in child rearing conclude, too, that offering a child a reward for good behavior only reduces the intrinsic satisfaction that the child might otherwise have had.

Of course, people have to earn a living, and we do want to be paid for our efforts. The essence of these conclusions is that you can't throw money at a person and expect a change in attitude and a rise in productivity—in fact, what you should expect is the exact opposite. In the classic *Tom Sawyer,* the perennial observer of human behavior Mark Twain opines, "There are wealthy gentlemen in England who drive four-horse passenger-coaches twenty or thirty miles on a daily line, in the summer, because the privilege costs them considerable money; but if they were offered wages for the service, that would turn it into work and then they would resign."

The optimum strategy is found in more precisely understanding the nuances involved. Psychologist Theresa Amabile distills the results of a 1984 study of motivation and reward with: *The more complex the activity, the more it's hurt by extrinsic reward.* These results, then, explain that for employees whose job entails mundane or even somewhat creative piecework, performance bonuses can be quite effective (as numerous other studies show). Conversely, employees whose job is more creative and complex will be happier and more productive when given freedom to choose their assignments and with salary not directly tied into performance.

Our solution emerges. Nothing in nature is identical to anything else; even identical twins have distinct fingerprints. We human beings derive such intense satisfaction from creative thought and action; the feeling we get is unparalleled. It locks in our attention and individuality. Have you ever noticed how much pleasure a small child gets from drawing a picture? Or even coloring?

We are driven to be unique, to express ourselves. When we are creating, we feel alive. To simply do, to not be creative in any way, has the potential for shutting us down. Creativity allows us to tap into the source of inspiration and impart our own sense of individuality to the world. Fewer things improve morale faster than allowing employees to put their own stamp, a piece of their uniqueness, onto their project and thereby imprint the task with intrinsic motivation.

## Paper or Plastic?

An experiment by economists Alexandre Mas and Enrico Moretti sought to learn whether productive employees slack off when working with unhurried coworkers, or vice versa—do the slackers pick up slack? Using scanner data from a large grocery chain, they measured cashier productivity and found a definitive increase when more productive employees were introduced into the mix. An analysis of the data proved that the increase was due not to a moral impetus of the slower cashier to try harder or form a burst of inspiration to be more proficient. Rather, productivity increased only when the slower cashiers were positioned so that their more efficient counterparts could see *them;* they did not want to be viewed as incompetent or purposely slacking off. The research concludes that "the optimal mix of workers in a given shift is the one that maximizes skill diversity."

See also:

- Chapter 21: *The Effortless Way to Make Difficult Changes without Creating Fearful, Frustrated, and Angry Employees*

# 5

## The Foolproof Strategy to Keep Any Employee from Stealing

*"Honesty is the best policy—when there is money in it."*

—Mark Twain (1835–1910)

Employee theft is big business. While statistics vary, employee theft and embezzlement costs organizations somewhere between $450 and $600 billion every year (giver or take a couple of billion). If industry-wide statistics don't mean much to you, perhaps these statistics will hit closer to home: More than fifty percent of all business bankruptcies are attributed to employee theft. Each year, employee theft will cause 20 percent of existing businesses and 30 percent of new businesses to fail. In fact, security industry experts estimate that 30 percent of all employees steal from their employers and that another 60 percent would steal, given sufficient motive and opportunity.

Often companies focus on protecting assets from external threats without realizing that their biggest security threat may be sitting right beside them in plain sight—their employees.

Conventional wisdom advocates control measures to predict and deter theft: preemployment integrity testing and background checks, sophisticated accounting control procedures, advanced surveillance procedures, and even sting operations. Yet, the data prove that only 1 in 35 employees is ever apprehended for stealing, and fewer than 10 percent of those are ever prosecuted.

Clearly, the control approach isn't enough. For starters, the trusted managers overseeing the control systems are often the ones doing the stealing. Swiss cooperative consulting network KPMG's "Profiles of a Fraudster Survey 2007" concluded that, in 55 percent of the theft cases involving top executives, there was no prior suspicion.

The KPMG survey points out that employers are often lulled into a false sense of comfort by relying on prehire background checks and internal controls and by believing that employee theft and fraud won't happen to them or that dishonesty will be spotted before it becomes a real problem. Although control systems can reduce theft opportunities, they don't predict dishonest behavior or motivate honest behavior.

---

### No Thieves Allowed

The smartest strategy for eliminating employee theft is the obvious one: hire people who won't steal. But how do you predict who will steal and who won't? Many companies use a practical integrity test such as the NEO Five-Factor Inventory (NFFI) to assess a job applicant's propensity for theft. The NFFI measures the five domains of adult personality, often referred to as the "Big-Five" traits. Longitudinal workplace behavior studies indicate that three Big-Five traits—conscientiousness, agreeableness, and neuroticism—can be used to predict theft, as well as absenteeism, tardiness, lack of cooperation, excessive breaks, and excess socializing.

---

A thorough prehire screening and interviewing process that probes a candidate's work history, personality characteristics, and ethical propensities can help an employer avoid predictable problems.

You may screen out known recidivist thieves, but screening new hires doesn't prevent your existing employees from stealing. The latest research in the field of industrial psychology offers the good news. Psychologist Lucy McClurg finds a factor we can control—perceived organizational support (POS)—to be a better predictor of theft than other attitudinal variables because "it more directly taps exchange relationships which have been shown to be important correlates of workplace theft" (McClurg and Butler 2006).

## What Is POS?

Employers and employees enter into an exchange relationship in which both tangibles, such as pay, and intangibles, such as satisfaction and commitment, are evaluated by employees for equity.

A 1998 study by Robert H. Moorman, Gerald L. Blakely, and Brian P. Niehoff demonstrated that POS is akin to a psychological contract. Employees exhibit good citizenship (meaning they won't steal) toward the organization in exchange for fair treatment, and employees feel obligated to their employer when their employer supports them.

## The Seven-Point Psychological Contract: Creating the Situational Edge

Seven additional factors go into the psychological mix.

**1. Managers as mirrors.** Organizational integrity starts at the top. In any given organization, overall employee ethics tend to mirror the ethics of management. Unethical managers give employees an excuse to rationalize stealing. If the supervisor fudges his expense account reporting, why shouldn't they? Therefore, supervisors need to set a clear example and display the highest degree of integrity when it comes to the little things that may fall into a gray area, such as office supplies, overseas phone calls, and overnight delivery.

**2. A formal code of ethics.** Believe it or not, some people are not exactly clear about what constitutes stealing and what is okay to take. Formal ethics training programs can provide models for employee moral judgments and reduce the need for the slippery slope of individual moral judgments, which removes some of the variance in individual behavior. A formal ethics program has the added benefit of complying with the Sarbanes-Oxley Act of 2002, which requires corporations to implement programs to reduce fraud in the workplace. Moreover, it actually works.

The 2002 Greenberg studies demonstrate that establishing a formal ethics program reduces theft. In the study, 270 customer service representatives were intentionally underpaid for completing a questionnaire after working hours on it and then told that payment came either from the company or from individual managers. Participants were made to believe that they could steal their payment and that the actual amount they stole would not be detected. Employees who had attained a conventional level of moral development from their organization's ethics program refrained from stealing money, whereas employees whose organizations had no ethics program did steal (Greenberg 2002).

**3. Equality for all.** Millie Kresevich (2007), a loss prevention specialist who has interviewed hundreds of employees caught stealing, says that "workers reacted to how they were treated and to the prevailing culture." Kresevich cites interviews with once-golden employees who ultimately stole from their companies to get back at management because they felt unappreciated or mistreated. Equity-sensitive employees sometimes steal in retaliation or to remedy a perceived pay inequity; workplace theft is closely associated with feelings of mistreatment by the employer.

**4. A vocal voice.** Give employees a say about matters that affect them. Help them commit to eliminating theft by letting them participate in goal setting. Solicit their input on how to curb theft, let them participate in determining how progress should be rewarded, and allow them to share in the savings. Establish specific shrinkage goals, measure progress, and offer progress feedback. Reward employees for any shrinkage reduction accomplishments.

**5. Getting to know your employees.** As organization size increases and degree of supervision decreases, theft increases. The Greenberg (2002) studies drew conclusions about proximal situations: Workers tended to steal more often in impersonal environments where the victim seemed distant. Participants who believed their payments came from individual managers refrained from stealing under any conditions.

**6. Providing alternatives to survival stealing.** When asked why he robbed banks, infamous bank robber Willie Sutton replied, "Because that's where the money is." Even employees in dire financial straits who are otherwise honest and hardworking may resort to theft as the last resort. Stealing may seem necessary for survival. Communicate to employees in advance that they should approach management for help rather than resort to theft. Help financially distressed individuals find financial counseling, or consider offering dependable, loyal employees short-term loans.

**7. A confidential reporting system.** Create an anonymous employee hotline and reward those who report theft; always reward the messenger who tells the truth, even if you don't particularly want to hear the message. Teach your employees what to look for. Employees are often in a better position to predict coworker theft than management. They have opportunities to observe dishonest coworkers in the trenches on a daily basis and are privy to unguarded coworker conversations that management isn't.

## What to Look for: The Seven Red Flags

In every mob movie, there's always one guy who doesn't heed the ubiquitous and predictable warning: Don't spend the money. He can't resist buying a flashy new car and lavishing furs and diamonds on his gum-chewing girlfriend—*right after the big heist*. If the obvious doesn't give him away, here's a sampling of what employees may know about a dishonest coworker that management doesn't:

1. That a coworker is acting differently right before or right after a theft.
2. That a coworker exhibits theft ideation, speaks of stealing money while supposedly just kidding around.
3. That, during a theft investigation, a coworker encouraged employees to stick together and not reveal information to investigators.
4. That a coworker has casually mentioned quitting his job, either before or after a theft occurred.
5. That a coworker's standard of living has risen dramatically, perhaps even suddenly, for no discernible reason.
6. That the coworker is responsible for excessive customer complaints of overcharging or inconsistent charging.
7. That a manager continually insists on handling routine clerical tasks that staff should be handling. Such individuals are either obsessive personalities who need to learn to delegate, covering for subordinates who are not doing their jobs, or stealing.

## Strategy 2: Thou Shalt Not Steal

For an amazingly valuable method that will reduce and possibly eliminate employee theft entirely, we're going to intertwine various principles of human nature into one complete strategy.

Because human beings have a strong need to be congruous with their self-concept, when we vocalize or in some way concretize an opinion—*regardless of whether we believe it to be true*—we usually come to support it in time. For instance, in a class assignment, students were chosen randomly to take different sides of an issue. After mock debates, students overwhelming accepted or at least sympathized with the position they had to defend—even when they did not believe it to be true in the first place.

Taylor and Booth-Butterfield (1993) asked a group of people to call for a taxi if, while they were drinking, they became impaired. Half of them also signed a petition against drunk driving, but the other half didn't. Those who signed the petition were much more likely to follow through with calling the taxi service once they were impaired than those who did not sign the petition. As unreal as it sounds, a simple petition created such a strong unconscious drive that even though the participants were quite inebriated, they stuck to their commitment.

A more intricate look at the underlying psychology divulges that when an inherent belief exists, we do not even need to publicly stipulate our position; rather, we need only *remind* ourselves of our thinking. This finding was revealed in a recent study that showed that given the opportunity to cheat for a little extra money, about 50 percent of the participants did so. Various theft-inhibiting approaches were tried, including increasing the fear of being caught. None significantly changed the level of dishonesty. Only one thing stopped cheating in its tracks.

The researcher states, "We found that getting people to contemplate their own standards of honesty (by recalling the Ten Commandments or signing an honor code) eliminated cheating completely" (Ariely 2008).

This study also exposed an amusing, if not unsettling, aspect of human nature. The author writes, "Perhaps most disturbing, we found that if payment was given in poker chips, which were exchanged for cash a few seconds later, the average level of cheating more than doubled." Casino operators, of course, recognize that people are more likely to risk losing chips than cash because of the perpetual, imperceptible, unconscious justification that it's not really money.

The potential, then, to rein in employee theft with some basic no-cost or low-cost tactics, is stunning. To deepen your employees' unconscious drive to remain trustworthy, employ any one or a combination of the following:

- Have employees sign a code of conduct and review it periodically.
- Have some of your (more questionable) employees read it to others and use them to work the petition.
- Make a video of your employees attesting to the importance of honesty.
- Hang a large and visible plaque attesting to these very virtues.

Do all of this in a very casual, nonthreatening way, and you will have ingrained in your employees' unconscious a very powerful attitude that stealing is not just wrong; rather, they are the type of person who does not steal.

See also:

- Chapter 14: *How to Spot a Bluff a Mile Away: The Ultimate Bluff Buster*
- Chapter 15: *Find Out if Your Employees Are Doing Drugs or Drinking on the Job with a 30-Second Nonaccusatory Conversation*

# Collect Money Owed, No Matter How Long It's Overdue

*"Creditors have better memories than debtors."*

—Benjamin Franklin (1706–1790)

The practice of debt collection is as old as the recorded history of business transactions. Practically every business in the world is plagued by bad debt. In January 2008, Moody's Investors Service forecast that the percentage of U.S. corporate bad debt to total debt would climb from its current 1 to 53 percent by the end of 2008.

Credit managers are often reluctant to launch an official collection process for fear of offending delinquent payers who were once model customers. This dilemma is particularly common among small business managers, who often know their customers by name. It can be tricky to determine which customers will have the resilience to overcome their financial woes and become model customers again, and which will spiral downward into bankruptcy.

But the problem remains: delinquent payables put your business at risk, and delinquent payables are particularly dangerous for small businesses, for whom cash flow is often critical.

Conventional collector industry wisdom holds that if you don't collect a debt within the first 90 days, you're unlikely to collect it without resorting to collection agencies, collection attorneys, and ultimately adversarial litigation. Not only is this assumption false, but the strong-arm tactics these third parties typically employ do not necessarily produce a better result.

If you have customers who are stretching payables weeks—or worse, *years*—beyond the due dates, it's time for a proactive, psychology-laden debt collection strategy.

## Understanding Debt Psychology

Debt psychology is influenced by a combination of the debtor's personality traits and the situational contingencies. Understanding the psychodynamic of how your debtor became a *delinquent* debtor will help you work out the best psychological approach to resolving the delinquency. Knowing the *why* makes the *how* possible.

Research conducted by Sonia Livingstone and Peter Lunt (1993) of the London School of Economics and Political Science explored three issues:

1. What discriminates debtors from nondebtors?
2. What determines how far into debt people get?
3. What determines how much of their debt people repay?

Interestingly, sociodemographic factors played a relatively minor role in personal debt and debt repayment. Disposable income did not differ between those in debt and those not in debt, although disposable income *did* predict how deeply in debt people were and was the most critical factor in determining debt repayment. But attitudinal factors—being *procredit* rather than *antidebt*, or seeing credit as useful but problematic—were the most important predictors of debt and debt repayments.

To summarize these findings, delinquent debtors typically fall into two categories: (1) those who want to pay but can't and (2) those who don't want to pay but can.

Therefore, our strategies include techniques that address the debtor who is apathetic as well the one who is cash-strapped. More often than not, the debtor has *some* cash on hand. Which creditor will get those limited dollars? Those who know how to apply psychological pressure in the right measure.

It goes without saying that it's better to perform this assessment before you extend credit—but we said it anyway. The more you know about the debtor's attitude toward debt, the better equipped you'll be to collect what you're owed. Does the debtor have a cavalier attitude about credit? Do you sense an underlying pathology that indicates this individual doesn't care whether you're ever repaid? This is the type of debtor you're more likely to end up having a problem with.

Conversely, was the debtor cautious about accumulating debt? Does the debtor see himself or herself as a moral individual who honors promises and satisfies obligations? If so, you have a higher probability of quick debt recovery and a higher likelihood of maintaining a positive relationship beyond the recovery of the debt.

### Casual Relationships

Auto insurance agencies now consider credit to be a critical rating factor in predicting which persons pose greater risk. Statistics demonstrate that the healthier your credit history, the less likely you are to file a claim against your auto or homeowners insurance policy—and the more likely you are to pay your insurance premium payments. Therefore, if your credit history is problematic, you may pay higher premiums than someone with an identical driving record; in fact, you may even be denied coverage altogether. The correlation between two seemingly unrelated factors gives us something to think about. Can we assume that individuals with less than stellar driving records may, in fact, turn out to be poor credit risks?

## Strategy 1: The Five-Point Approach

**1. Always insert one degree of distance.** Point the finger at a third party for your collection efforts—your CPA, your business manager, your CEO, your lawyer. "My business manager requires that we don't let accounts remain unpaid beyond 45 days."

Inserting one degree of distance between your collection efforts and your personal relationship with the debtor helps preserve a pliable, amicable relationship, which sets the table for successful negotiation and ultimately successful resolution. This transforms your role into that of a sort of mediator, which helps neutralize the debtor's frustration and embarrassment during those difficult conversations and leaves plenty of room for you to empathize with the debtor's predicament.

**2. Heed the elements of style.** The tone of the message is as important as what you say. Leonard Sklar, customer relations consultant and author of *The Check Is Not in the Mail* (1990), recommends softening the blow of the "you must pay" message with lines such as: "You've been a good customer and I would really feel terrible if anything I said offended you. I know times are tough right now, but I have to say that I want you to pay what you owe us." Interestingly, Sklar has found that such statements even work on people who use the same approach with their own customers.

**3. Make it personal.** Find a tactful way to point out the debtor's social obligation, especially if you personally went out on a limb for this customer, perhaps vouching for the customer's creditworthiness or extending special favors, such as a discount or a higher credit limit. Load your language with words designed to trigger an emotional response. The word *promise*, for example, is more emotionally charged than *debt* or *outstanding balance*. It carries a host of unconscious connotations and delivers a more powerful psychological punch than *obligation* or *liability*.

Politicians well understand the power of words to influence attitude and behavior. People are more comfortable hearing about a *military action* than about a *war*, even though they mean the same thing. We would rather hear of *collateral damage* than be told that *civilian property was accidentally destroyed;* we are not as disturbed by hearing of *friendly fire* as we would be to hear what it really means— *our soldiers shot at our own forces.* And of course, watching the morning news, we are less moved being told of *casualties* than we would be if the reporter said what that meant: *deaths.*

**4. Never express contempt.** If you express disrespect, you've just quashed any hope of reasonable negotiation. Humans are exceptionally good at sensing contempt, even in phone conversations. Contempt is closely related to disgust, a complete rejection that few humans can bear. Expressing contempt says: "You are worthless." While not a productive attitude in itself, you unwittingly engage the law of expectation against your favor.

To a great extent, people do what you expect them to do, and this mind-set fosters a belief that you don't expect to be paid.

Parenthetically, this is true for personal as well as professional scenarios and situations. John Gottman (2005), a psychologist at the University of Washington, studied more than 2,000 married couples over two decades. He discovered four patterns that can be used to predict—*with a staggering 94 percent accuracy*—which relationships will succeed and which will fail. The four attitudes that predict the dissolution of a relationship are defensiveness, stonewalling, criticism, and contempt, which Gottman calls the Four Horsemen of the Apocalypse.

The most damaging of these four attitudes, by far, is contempt. Gottman's research showed that once conversations start spiraling downward, the relationship becomes irreconcilable 94 percent of the time.

How do you know when you're crossing the line? These behaviors are indicators:

- Attacking the individual's sense of self; deliberate psychological abuse
- Hurling insults or name-calling
- Engaging in hostile humor, sarcasm, or mockery
- Showing body language such as sneering or rolling your eyes

---

### Keep It Real

Don't employ cheap stunts, and don't misrepresent your power; for example, don't insinuate that failure to pay will result in imprisonment. *Unless of course, after pulling the initial credit application, you find something was fudged.* In this instance, then, reminding him that his unintentional oversight might be construed as fraud uncomfortably shifts the conversation and relationship, but also may prompt payment.

---

**5. Not business as usual.** What if you found yourself a quarter short for that all-important cup of coffee? If you were brave enough to ask a stranger for change, what amount do you think would be best to ask for, a quarter, 37 cents, or some spare change? Research shows that people are most likely to respond if you ask for 37 cents—in fact, twice as many—than those asked for a quarter.

Naturally, digging out a quarter from their pockets or purse would be easier than trying to find more, so why do people not respond as compassionately when asked for a simple quarter? Because when they were asked for the 37 cents, the request was considered more carefully. Asking for an odd amount makes people actually stop and think about *you* and your needs (Santos, Leve, and Pratkanis 1991).

The main objective is to get the debtor to actually *hear* your request for money before summarily dismissing it. Asking for a routine and ordinary payment amount makes the request easier to initially disregard and to later forget.

---

### Elicit Commitment

A postdated check is a postdated promise that commits the debtor to the next payment. **Collection industry statistics indicate that 98 percent of postdated checks will be valid when deposited.** An emotional commitment is created (based on *cognitive dissonance*) the minute a person postdates a check—*this one is important*, he thinks to himself; he then feels obligated to follow through. In addition to this psychological factor, most delinquent debtors are hesitant to add fraud charges to their woes.

---

## Strategy 2: Reciprocity and Confirmation

Have you ever been in a situation where someone does something for you and you feel uncomfortable unless you can pay him back in some way? We know we don't *have* to, but we are often uneasy until we can reciprocate. Why? Because it creates a sense of dependency.

Any side that *gives in* to the other creates a sense of dependency in the other side. To regain a sense of independence, the other party is driven to give something back. Therefore, any concession that one side makes pulls the other—unconsciously—closer to the middle.

But a sense of dependency already exists, you say? He owes me money! No. In his mind, you haven't done anything *for* him; rather, he's done something *to you*. Do you see the difference? If you accidentally step on a person's foot, a sense of dependency is not created, as this person didn't do anything for you. Yes, you feel bad, but only because of what you did to him. However, if we had some absurd, urgent, obsessive need to step on another's foot and this person allowed us to do so, then we have created a true psychological dependency.

To put this dynamic to work for you, if you go out on a limb for him *now*, in spite of his tardiness, you will create a strong uneasiness. Because you are not obligated, let alone expected, to help him, the gesture elevates itself to a genuine emotional debt that he will feel the necessity to repay—vis-à-vis the actual financial debt.

But it gets better! Researcher Angela Lipsitz and others (1989) found that ending a blood-drive reminder call with "We'll count on seeing you then, okay?" and then pausing for response, raised their show-up rate from *62 to 81 percent*. This single, simple confirmation increased the rate by an incredible 20 percent.

When the debtor issues a verbal agreement to make a payment, be sure that your reply asks for a *verbal confirmation*. This will solidify his internal consistency and increase his commitment to follow through.

---

### Ace in the Hole

The best defense is a strong offense. Try employing this idea in advance of any slow-pay problem. Numerous studies show that any small gift—particularly one that is not only unexpected but *personalized*, that is, reflecting the recipient's hobby or interests—generates an amazing amount of goodwill and shifts the relationship to one that is more personal and harder to ignore.

---

## Strategy 3: Try the Silent Treatment with a Twist

Have your previous collection attempts failed? Try the silent treatment. You may think of it as childish or overly simple, but it works.

Call your debtor, explain that you're calling about the delinquent account, and simply wait for a response. Don't say another word. Don't threaten, warn, or embellish. You may be greeted by a lengthy silence on the other end of the line. If so, wait it out.

You'll find, sometimes, that your silence elicits a gush of information about your debtor's cash situation and intent to pay. Some will be so startled they promise a payment immediately; others will tell you their life stories. Just listen. Let them talk. Sometimes people just need to be heard.

The key here is to be *persistent, yet highly respectful;* in time, the debtor will begin to feel bad for *you.* Imagine getting a call once every few days that sounded like "Hi, Chris, I'm sorry to bother you again; I know how busy you are. I wanted to know if you might be able to send me $47.66 this week? We're really in a cash crunch ourselves."

Delinquent debtors can and do become good customers again, and those delinquent customers who appreciated the way you handled them when they were down on their luck may just be the most loyal customers you'll ever have.

---

### Establish a Clear, Written Credit Policy for All Customers

Provide all customers with a written credit policy when you extend credit to them. Notify existing customers, as well, if you've been remiss in formalizing your credit policy in the past. Acknowledge their model credit history and explain that, while you're not concerned about their creditworthiness, you simply haven't communicated your credit policy as clearly as you should have and feel that you owe it to every customer to ensure that there will never be misunderstandings. A written policy should spell out payment terms, payment method options, discounts for prompt payment, penalties for late payment, and when accounts go to collection. Soften the overall tone by including your satisfaction and refund policy and— always—your appreciation for their business.

# Strategy 4: Advance, Then Retreat

Researchers asked college students on the street if they would volunteer to be an unpaid counselor for juvenile delinquents two hours a week for a two-year period. No one said yes. But then, before the subjects walked away, they were asked if they would agree to take these same kids on a two-hour trip to the zoo. *Fifty percent* of the students said yes. However, when students were asked about chaperoning the zoo trip without first being asked the larger request, only *seventeen percent* agreed (Cialdini et al. 1975).

This tactic is a spin-off on the previously discussed rule of reciprocity. Ask the debtor for a much larger request than he is likely to agree to. And then after he refuses, you ask for something smaller— the amount that you can really live with.

The psychology here is threefold: (1) After the other person makes a concession, we feel the need to reciprocate; (2) we don't want to be perceived as unyielding and unreasonable; and (3) we want to think of ourselves as good, and so we seek to get rid of that bad taste of not helping by doing something easier and less demanding.

## A Personal Touch

When you send out the bill, add a personal touch. Psychologist and researcher Randy Garner sought to discover whether sticking a yellow Post-it note with a few personalized words on it would make a difference when he sent out requests for information. More than 75 percent of those who received a request with just a hand-written "thank you" or "I appreciate your time" Post-it note replied, compared with 36 percent of those who received a typed cover letter only. The perception that someone had taken the trouble to personalize a request made all the difference (Garner, 2005). You can still do more. A separate study showed that both undergraduates and college professors filled out and returned questionnaires at a higher frequency rate when the name on the cover letter was similar to their own (Garner, 2005). To boost your response rate, give thought to assigning pen names to those in collections.

See also:

- Chapter 1: *The Psychological Strategy to Gain Ironclad Loyalty: Never Lose an Employee, Customer, Client, or Patient Again*
- Chapter 17: *Sway The Room: From Jury Rooms to Board Rooms, How One Voice Can Change the Choir*
- Chapter 18: *Master the Art of Charisma with the Complete Psychological Formula for Instant Likability*

# 7

## Turn a Saboteur into Your Greatest Ally

*"In the end, we will remember not the words of our enemies, but the silence of our friends."*
—Martin Luther King, Jr. (1929–1968)

Have you ever found yourself in a situation where someone seemed bent on sabotaging you, and you're not even sure why? Here's the general rule: If a person dislikes you without good reason, it's not that he doesn't like *you*. It's that he doesn't like himself very much. You give respect, so if you don't respect yourself, what do you have to give?

A person who doesn't like himself has low self-esteem, a damaging psychological deficit that becomes a lens through which all experiences are filtered. This distorted perception ultimately instills one or more of these beliefs:

1. *He believes you dislike him.* Perhaps he misinterpreted an expression on your face, or something you said or did. Perhaps you've unintentionally neglected or ignored him, or at least not given him your full attention. It doesn't take much for a person with low self-esteem to become convinced that you don't like him. Since he doesn't like himself much, he naturally assumes—on an unconscious level—that other people must not like him either.

2. *He feels threatened by you.* A fragile ego is envious and jealous. You may remind him of what he wants but doesn't have. To reconcile these feelings of inadequacy, he imprints you with negative traits, then dislikes you for having them.

3. *He sees in you the traits that he dislikes in himself.* Hence he dislikes *you* because you remind him of what he dislikes about himself, albeit unconsciously.

## Strategy 1: Turning Enemies into Friends—Nine Simple Rules

Keeping the saboteur from ruining things is easier than you think. These nine rules are straightforward and fast-acting, and they'll work in just about every relationship dynamic—in both your business and personal life.

## Rule 1: Establish Reciprocal Liking

Ever had the experience of having someone you don't particularly like pay you a huge compliment or ask your advice? It's incredibly hard to dislike someone who not only likes you but *respects* you, isn't it? You're suddenly forced to reevaluate your feelings toward him. Suddenly, you view him more favorably. After all, you don't want to believe he's foolish to like and respect you, since he thinks so highly of you! No, we'd prefer to adjust our thinking about the other person and conclude that maybe he's not such a bad guy after all. This is called *reciprocal affection*, which simply means that we're inclined to like, admire, and respect someone once we find out that they like, admire, and respect us.

To enact this law, tell a third party (perhaps a mutual friend) what you honestly *like* and *respect* about your saboteur—perhaps express genuine admiration for something she's accomplished or something she stands for. Once your comment makes its way to her, you can just sit back and watch what happens. You'll be amazed at how quickly she's converted into an ally. Whether it's a coworker, boss, assistant, neighbor, sibling, child, or your car mechanic, remember: *everyone needs to feel appreciated.*

Now, maybe you're wondering, Why can't I just tell her myself? You could, but you run the risk of her suspecting that you're being insincere or just trying to manipulate her into liking you. The secret behind the tactic's effectiveness is that when we hear something from a third party, we rarely question the veracity of what we're told, especially if it's something we *want* to hear.

## Rule 2: Show Genuine Enthusiasm When You Greet the Person

A smile can work miracles, especially with a saboteur. Whenever you greet him, make a point to do it with as genuine a smile as you can muster. This sends the message that you're pleased to see her and makes her feel better about herself, and you. Likewise, a warm smile will make it harder for him to feel threatened by you, much less think that you don't like him.

## Rule 3: Be Supportive

If you learn that your saboteur has made a mistake, reassure her that such mistakes could happen to anyone, and tell her she shouldn't be so hard on herself. Whatever you do, don't criticize or condemn. In the cases where she's having a disagreement with another person (which probably happens often), *defend her* if you believe there's merit to her side of the argument. When the two of you have a disagreement, try to remember that there's no reward for being right and for proving that you're smarter than she is. You won't gain a thing. If you acknowledge that she's made a good, insightful, or interesting point, however—if even if you have to disagree—you have everything to gain.

## Rule 4: Give Your Saboteur the Benefit of the Doubt

If you expect the worst from a saboteur, you're going to get it. Just as she views you through a distorted lens, so will you be viewing her. If she does something that *seems* to reflect a lack of respect for you, cut her some slack. If she borrows something without permission or exits a meeting that you're conducting early and without explanation, let your first assumption be that she had a good reason. If you inquire about the incident, don't interrogate. Don't be accusatory or argumentative. Even if her motivation was less than pure, your reaction this time can change her actions the next time.

## Rule 5: Let Her Know You Appreciate Her

Too often, it seems that the only time we say something nice to someone is when we need to make amends because we've done something bad. You'll be amazed at how much better you'll get along with someone if you become proactive about expressing your appreciation: *Thank you. I appreciate what you did for me. Thank you for being there.* A few simple words of appreciation in reserve are worth a thousand after the fact if problems later arise in the relationship. You're banking a goodwill investment that will continue to yield high returns.

## Rule 6: The Art of Listening

Imagine having a conversation with someone while his cell phone rings constantly, but he chooses not to answer it. You might say, "Do you need to get that?" But he simply says, "Don't worry about it. I'm interested in talking to you right now." Wouldn't this make you feel good?

Being half-listened to—or perhaps more accurately, half-ignored—makes us feel diminished and unimportant. Perhaps you've had the experience of speaking with someone at a party and become aware that his eyes are roving the room behind you, even as he's pretending to be listening to you.

Listening—really listening—is about respect. If someone is talking to you, it's disrespectful to listen with one ear or keep one eye trained on the TV, computer, or newspaper. Giving your undivided attention to someone is a sign of respect. It might seem like a little thing, but it's the kind of little thing that really affects how well two people get along.

## Rule 7: Give Her a Chance to Contribute to Your Life

There is no greater way to bond with someone than to let her be a part of your life and invest herself in you. Ask a saboteur for advice and feedback when you think she might have something worthwhile to contribute. Allowing her to *give* makes her feel good, and this sharing environment helps you grow closer.

Studies in human nature show us that people actually dislike others *more* after doing them harm. Why? When we harm someone—either on purpose or by accident—we are unconsciously driven to dislike the person in an attempt to reduce what's known as *cognitive dissonance*. (Cognitive dissonance theory holds that we feel uneasy when we do something that is inconsistent with how we see ourselves. To resolve this inner conflict, we rationalize and justify our behavior so that it can remain consistent with our self-concept.) The internal conflict created is: Why did I do this to this person? The rationalization must then become: It must be because I really don't like him and he deserves it! Otherwise, you must be a bad person or, at the least, careless. We must be able to live with ourselves.

This principle works in reverse, too. We like someone more after doing something nice for her. If we do someone a favor, we're likely to have positive feelings toward that person.

If you can get her to do *you* a small favor, she'll have kind, warm feelings toward you. Often, in an attempt to get someone to like us, we make the mistake of doing nice things for her. And while she may appreciate your kindness and think you're a nice person, it doesn't necessarily make her like you more, even if she now views you as *more likable*. Your goal, remember, is for her to have kind feelings toward you, not just to believe that you're a kind person. So, your goal will be accomplished by her doing something nice for you, not by your doing something nice for her.

## Rule 8: Share Yourself

Even if the relationship is not a personal relationship, let this person into your life a bit—share something personal, something that has emotional resonance. You may find this easier to accomplish on common ground, and you can find this space with almost anyone. Some of us are naturally expressive about our personal lives, and some of us are more reserved. If you don't always find it easy to share your personal feelings, you may discover that this exercise greatly enhances all your relationships, whether business or personal.

Once mutual respect is established, almost any minor transgression or oversight by either person will be filtered through the mutual respect lens. Future misunderstandings and miscommunications will be perceived as honest, unintentional mistakes, rather than as intentional damage. You'll find that situations that might have otherwise ballooned into problems will resolve themselves.

## Rule 9: Focus on the Good

Numerous studies prove what our own experiences have already shown us—a person intuitively senses whether we like him, even without a single word being exchanged. When you speak with him, mentally focus on his positive trait(s), and he will sense that you like him—and, in turn, he will like you.

It happened that a butcher became very angry at the rabbi of his city for rendering a decision that the meat of a cow the butcher wanted to sell was not kosher. The decision cost the butcher great financial loss. In his rage, the butcher devised a scheme to murder the rabbi. On a pretext, he had the rabbi travel with him on a lonely road. Along the way, the butcher took out his sharp knife and wanted to kill the rabbi.

When the rabbi saw that nothing he could say would make a difference, he started to mentally focus on all of the positive qualities and attributes of the butcher that he was familiar with. Suddenly, there was a remarkable transformation. In the midst of the rabbi's thinking about the virtues of the butcher, the butcher changed his mind. With a strong feeling of love, the butcher—with tears in his eyes—kissed the rabbi and begged his forgiveness.

President Abraham Lincoln has been quoted as saying, "I don't like that man very much, so I am going to try to get to know him better." Not to be outdone, Benjamin Franklin is quoted with "Search others for their virtues and others will search for yours."

The mother of a mass murderer can love her son, because that is what she chooses to focus on. If we look for the good in another, we will find it. And when we do, our face will shine with the light that reflects these positive and warm feelings.

## Don't Shoot the Messenger

Relationships are a very common area in which people often miss the message and focus on the messenger. We must understand the larger picture and ask ourselves: What lesson can I learn from this person?

When we are blatantly correct in a specific instance, we usually make an excuse as to why we have no responsibilities in that situation. The prerequisite for growing in any area is not to blame, or to be enraged at the injustice of the situation, but to ask oneself practically: What is the responsible thing for me to do right now?

It is only when we respond to another's cruelty with like that we move to a mode of dependence, and so pain. There is no way to get around this. Guilt will seep in, our ego engages to fortify our actions and our beliefs, and all the while, our self-esteem and emotional well-being slowly melt. While we are in blame mode, we are also not solution oriented and therefore cannot see, let alone investigate, ways to improve the situation.

See also:

- Chapter 9: *Managing Difficult People: The Psychology Behind Royal Pains*
- Chapter 16: *Bully-Proof Yourself and Your Office*
- Chapter 18: *Master the Art of Charisma with the Complete Psychological Formula for Instant Likability*
- Chapter 19: *The Amazing Method for Getting Along with People Who Are Emotionally Unwell*

# Get Back Any Customer You've Lost, No Matter Why They Left

*"Your most unhappy customers are your greatest source of learning."*

—Bill Gates (1955– ),
*Business @ the Speed of Thought*

Even with exceptional customer service, every business experiences customer loss. Although it may seem easier to write off a lost customer and tell yourself there are other fish in the sea, it is often more cost-effective to win back customers than it is to sell your product or service to a brand-new customer.

Naturally, retaining customers is being certain that you understand the needs of your customers. Ask them why they choose you over your competitors. Find out what they like best and least about your company. Get suggestions and complaints about how things should be done and what needs to be added to your business. Once the customer is out the door, you need to shift tactics to get them back as soon as possible.

Most corporate executives and business owners immediately assume that most customers leave their company due to price issues; however, that is not the case. When asked why they stopped buying from a particular company or using a specific service, *a vast majority stated that they left because they were treated poorly or indifferently.*

Any time a customer leaves, if it's not about money, then it's about ego (a real or perceived lack of respect, time, and attention). Any other objection or claim is simply not likely to be true. An ego-satiating approach is in order.

## Apples and Oranges

A local supermarket has lost many formerly loyal customers to a large chain store that has moved to the area. Price cuts and marketing campaigns have not seemed to help the matter. Upon surveying some of the former customers, they find that the passive nature of the store's staff was the reason many were so anxious to make the change to another establishment.

> The management worked to develop a more customer-oriented atmosphere and invited the entire community to see the changes that had been made, resulting in a large number of customers returning.

## Strategy 1: The Five-Point Plan to Win Back Any Customer

### 1. Time of Contact

When we are in a good mood, we tend to be more optimistic, more open to a change of mind, and more receptive to hearing out others. People who are in a good mood are statistically more likely to purchase a lottery ticket than when they are in a foul mood.

You may notice yourself that when you're in a good mood, things don't get to you as much as when you're already upset over something. When you're in a bad mood, even the slightest annoyance can get under your skin. The psychology at play is that being in a good mood temporarily boosts self-esteem, which is self-love. This diminishes the ego, and when the ego moves out of the way, our natural desire to connect, relate, and empathize emerges. Think of mood as the shadow of self-esteem. The shift is not permanent, but it has a real, transitory effect on how we see ourselves and our lives.

So be sure to make your approach *only* when your former customer is unrushed and in an upbeat mood. Very often, and much to our detriment, we do the exact opposite; we reach out to a person when one of us is angry, annoyed, or rushed, and we expect somehow to have a meaningful and productive discussion. The other person's receptivity hinges as much on the timing of your message as it does on the actual words you use. That said, words matter.

### 2. He's at the Controls

The main reason this person may be reluctant to hear you out is a reasonable belief that if he gives you that commitment to listen, it will be more difficult to say no to any request. It's also felt that once he agrees to listen to you, that somehow he will lose some of his power. To counteract this reluctance, communicate the following themes:

- He is in total control of the situation. At any time, he can choose to end the conversation, and he will not be begged to hear your entire presentation, nor have his arm twisted to give you another chance.
- The conversation will be quick, easy, and simple, not some long, drawn-out affair. Ask for something such as four minutes (the odd time works in your favor, as previously discussed) and stick to it.
- There are no required commitments. Again, it's about control. If he knows that he will not be forced into a sales pitch, he will be more willing to acquiesce. You simply want the opportunity to explain your side. Regardless of what he decides, you will politely and respectfully accept his wishes. We all like to *try* things, but few of us like to commit. Advertisers know that the word *try* and phrases that imply a lack of commitment are highly persuasive: "Try our new product." "Test-drive the redesigned car." "Thirty-day no-risk trial offer." So don't ask for the customer to come back to you lock, stock, and barrel. Rather, ask that you be allowed to earn back their business. Ask for him to try the new you, in some small way, and take your company out for a test spin.

---

### A New Role

Before you even begin to ask him to reconsider your position, give him further information. No one wants to be thought of as indecisive, meaning that if he changes his mind before you give him any new information, he may be seen as, or believe himself to be, inconsistent in his thinking. Instead, offer additional relevant information or remind him of some strong points he might have forgotten. By doing it this way, you will give him the power to make a new decision based on the additional information rather than based on simply changing his mind.

---

## 3. Dilute Impact and Reassure

If it's practical, you want to explain how the company's actions were not unique to her and were a part of a larger problem. This helps to dilute the impact. For example, let's say that your former customer was upset and left because shipping was delayed on their new product. If your customer discovers that while his shipment was late by two weeks, most of your other customers' orders were delayed twice that time and that you made every effort to prioritze his shipment because of how valuable he is to you, he might have a different take on things. He no longer takes it personally and is likely to assign your company's actions to something out of your control, out of the ordinary.

To further reinforce your commitment to making sure that this issue does not recur, propose a bold guarantee. Offering him a luke-warm discount should he again be inconvenienced will do absolutely nothing, except annoy him more. Instead, *a 100 percent discount will surely shock him into reconsidering.* Of course, the nature of your business and the terms determine what is feasible. The overall objective, however, is to convey in the strongest possible way that you will do everything in your power, and beyond, to make sure that he is treated like royalty.

Many corporations find that creating a president's liaison, or something to that effect, gives customers the feeling that their account is extremely important. When you lose a client, the caller should be the highest ranking person in your firm that is possible. Again, if it's not about money, it's about ego, and the more you show him how important he is to your company, the greater your chances that he will return. All people have a need to feel important; it is one of the strongest urges felt by humans. When dealing with customers on this level, you want to make them feel as if winning them back is the most important task of your career and that your business will just not be the same without them.

## 4. Reshape the Self-Concept

In a pioneering study, Read Montague of the Baylor College of Medicine gave subjects the Pepsi challenge—asked participants to sample both Pepsi and Coke and then state their preference—while viewing their reactions with a functional magnetic resonance imaging (FMRI) scanner. The findings were fascinating. Subjects typically found Pepsi tastier, which was confirmed visually by the FMRI when the brain's reward center lit up. Nevertheless, the Coke branding was so strong, as it related to their self-concepts, that they vocalized support for it instead. The power of branding is so strong that people will buy and use a product they like less than a readily available alternative if they *identify with it* and see themselves as that kind of person.

Human beings have a strong need to be congruent with their concepts of themselves. We call this the *self-concept*, and it encompasses the way we see ourselves, our social abilities and character, our physical body image (the way we perceive it), and the way we think.

Although there are a variety of ways to reshape a person's self-concept, language is one of the simplest and most effective means. Let's take an example. A salesman wants to make sure that one of his vendors will keep doing business with him, even though he's made several mistakes on the bills.

*"I realize that we made an error on your invoice again. I appreciate that you are the kind of person who is willing to overlook mistakes and give people a chance to make it up to you. I've always respected that about you."*

A few simple sentences can reshape the vendor's self-concept and your relationship to include the definition of someone who believes that of him. This shift makes him want to live up to the image that you have of him, and he is driven subconsciously to fulfill your expectations. You see him in a certain positive light, and he then needs to protect this positive image. If he remained resistant to a reasonable request—in this case, to give your company another try—he would risk having to reevaluate his self-concept.

## 5. We Owe It All to You

When following up with a lost client, you need to get as many details as possible. Ask exactly what led them to leave your company. If a specific incident caused them to walk out the door, find out the who, what, when, and why of what happened. Spend time to investigate how to avoid this situation from happening again, and put a system into place irrespective of his agreeing to come back. Doing so shows that you recognize the seriousness of the mistake. Now the revelation.

Let him know—if, of course, it is true—that these changes were initiated as a result of his unfortunate experience with your company, and thank him for being a catalyst for improving your services. This creates an interesting psychological phenomenon because now others—your company and customers—are benefiting from his loss. He is thereby unconsciously motivated to get in on the action; why should he not benefit, too?

---

### Be Proactive

A well-known women's clothing retailer has sales associates keep a file card on each regular customer. They record contact information, as well as information on what the client purchases during a visit and the dates of these purchases. Management regularly goes through these cards and pulls those of customers who have not made a purchase in some time. They can then contact that customer and determine if she encountered a problem at the store that needs to be addressed; or that she has stopped shopping with them for an unrelated reason.

---

## Strategy 2: Okay, You're Right, but Do It My Way Anyway

Instead of making an issue about fair or not, right and wrong, simply ask the person to come back to your company *as a favor.* Now he will feel as if he's doing something nice—an act of kindness for you—as opposed being persuaded. This completely changes the psychological dynamics because he can still be right *and* do what you want anyway.

By trying to sway him, you have two obstacles: his ego and his intellect. In this way, you avoid engaging his ego because you are not telling him he is wrong, he does not have to defend his position, and he can objectively consider your request.

Don't make the mistake of trying to defend your company's position if he is not willing to hear you out in a fair way. You see, it is impossible for him to argue with someone who asks him to do something merely because he is asked to do it. There is no reason. You don't have to convince him of anything, and so his usual defenses are ineffective at rebuffing your request—you are in full agreement with him. You messed up, and he has no good reason to come back, other than as a favor to you.

From a subconscious, emotional standpoint, instead of feeling like he's giving in (which is a weakening of power), he is giving to you, which makes him feel good. It is the difference between giving a donation and being mugged. In both cases, money is moving from one person to another, but one instance is empowering, and the other is emotionally draining.

By eliminating the power struggle, you put him in a position of power, and this is what he needs the most.

Indeed, another powerful psychological force is in play. This technique moves the other person's perception from an economic model to a social model. In *Predictably Irrational* (2008), Dan Ariely recounts that when the AARP asked some lawyers to offer a range of simple services to needy retirees for $30 an hour, they overwhelmingly refused. The request was then changed, but instead of being offered a higher fee, the lawyers were asked to offer the same services for *free*. The result? Nearly all of them agreed.

When presented with the initial offer of $30, the lawyers made an economic decision and concluded that it was not worth it. However, when the fee was removed altogether, the decision moved into the social realm, where we do things for other people merely because it is a nice or right thing to do—not because it makes sense financially. By asking for a favor, you jump ship to the social model, where your leverage, in this instance, far exceeds the soured economic model.

In addition, you can increase the effectiveness of this strategy by further engaging his sense of empathy. This is best accomplished if the other party feels that our plight is not due to apathy, ignorance, or incompetence. Most people don't hesitate when an animal is injured and needs care; because animals cannot inflict pain and injury on themselves, we know that whatever injury the animal has was perpetrated by an outside force. This is in direct contrast with the attitude of many people as they pass the homeless in the streets and assume they are drunks or drug addicts who are themselves at fault for the situation they are in. In instances where the person is not directly responsible, we feel empathy because we see him as a victim—in our case, just like the customer, rather than the cause of his own inconvenience or troubles.

To whatever degree is remotely appropriate, share a personal and emotional story about yourself. As our own experience bears out, people love stories; in fact, ironic as it is, studies show that we pay closer attention and more readily believe information when it comes in story form. Revealing that you have financial troubles or that your dog died is much less effective than taking the time to put the situation into the context of a story or anecdote (Shermer 1997).

Specifically, your story does three things: (1) It shows that you trust him enough to share such personal information about yourself, (2) it makes you more sympathetic, and (3) it enacts the law of reciprocity. Since you have opened up and shared yourself, he feels the need to reciprocate by giving to you the one thing you want—his business.

---

### The Assistant Holds the Key

A 2000 survey by Menlo Park, California–based Office Team showed that 91 percent of executives consider their assistant's opinion a principal factor in the employee selection process. But it doesn't stop there. From hiring to firing, from buying to selling, the role of the assistant is becoming ever more influential. Developing rapport and cultivating a cordial and friendly relationship with this key person may give you the leverage you need, should it come time to woo back this client.

---

See also:

- Chapter 1: *The Psychological Strategy to Gain Ironclad Loyalty: Never Lose an Employee, Customer, Client, or Patient Again*

# 9

# Managing Difficult People: The Psychology Behind Royal Pains

*"When dealing with people, remember you are not dealing with creatures of logic, but creatures of emotion."*

—Dale Carnegie (1888–1955)

E very workplace has one, and some have more than one. According to Robert D. Ramsey, those in supervisory positions spend an estimated 18 percent of their time coping with personality conflicts that erupt among employees (*Interpersonal Conflicts*, 2005). That amounts to an estimated two months per year spent on complete and utter nonsense.

Your best weapon to deal with these personalities is to understand exactly how and why these people came to be who they are. Armed with this knowledge, you'll be able to more effectively get difficult people to fall in line with the company line.

## Psychology at Work

To be happy, have good relationships, and be psychologically balanced, people have to feel good about themselves. This feeling of self-worth is what we call *self-esteem*.

How does a person gain self-esteem? We all make choices as we go through our daily lives. When we *choose* to do what we believe is the right thing, we feel good about ourselves, and when we do what we know is wrong, we often feel guilt, embarrassment, and shame.

But let's back up for just a moment. When you make a decision in life, any decision, you always have one or a combination of three underlying motivations:

1. You can choose what *feels* good.
2. You can choose what makes you *look* good.
3. You can choose to do what *is* good or right.

The first two motivations chip away at our self-esteem, and the third makes us feel good about ourselves and who we are. Here's a closer look at how and why this happens.

When you choose to do something merely because it *feels* good—even though you know that it may be wrong, your self-image erodes. For instance, when you overeat, you don't feel good about yourself, and afterward you may even feel guilty and angry. Or if you sleep late when you had wanted to get an early start, you may become annoyed with yourself. When you make a decision that goes against your true inner desire—to eat well or get up early—you are, in effect, a slave to your cravings. Hence, you are not free or independent.

Now when you do something merely because it makes you *look* good but you know it is wrong, you are not living for yourself but only for an image. When you are driven by ego, you do things that project the right image, and you become consumed with approval, control, and respect. Your choices are not based on what is good but rather on what makes you look good. When you live to support an image, you are reliant on others to feed your ego. This makes you increasingly vulnerable, unstable, and dependent.

However, when you make a choice to do what is right, you feel good about yourself. This is because *to feel good, you must do good*, not what feels good or looks good. Only when you are able to choose responsibly are you in charge of your life; only then do you gain self-esteem. Then you're emotionally free, and you feel good about who you are.

## Here's How It All Fits Together

The part of us that seeks respect from others is called the *ego*. The ego is a projection of how we want and need the world to see us. With low self-esteem (meaning the ego is in charge), when we get good or positive feedback, we feel good about ourselves. When we don't, we feel less good about who we are.

The bottom line is that the more self-esteem we have, the less dependent we are on others to make us feel good. The less we like ourselves, the more dependent we are on others to nourish us emotionally.

This love that we need comes in the package of respect. If other people respect us, then we feel that we can respect ourselves as we convert their respect of us into *self-love*. Self-esteem and ego both pivot on *self-respect*. We need it from somewhere, and if we don't get it from ourselves, we demand it from others.

If you have low self-esteem, then that means, by definition, that you do not feel in control. And the less control we have over ourselves, the more we try to control the lives of others, and become indignant when the world does not unfold according to our expectations. You will not sit idly by and let someone come along and rob you of your last few remaining drops of independence and power, of feeling in control. *If you just glanced at this paragraph, please reread it, as it is at the foundation of all interpersonal conflicts.*

Any situation that you deem directly disrespectful, or that robs you of your self-respect by taking away your power, forces you to react negatively. If you feel in control and hence have self-esteem, then you are *not* going to respond with anger. The higher a person's self-esteem, the less angry he becomes in any given negative situation.

## Why Is Anger the Emotional Response?

When we do not get respect from others, we get angry because it hurts how *we need to see ourselves*. It cuts off our food supply—our nourishment for the psyche. The emotional response to this loss of control is fear. And the response to fear—the ego's attempt to compensate for the loss—is anger. At the root of all negative emotions—envy, lust, jealousy, and especially anger—is fear. At the root of fear is low self-esteem. This is why angry people have low self-esteem. This is why they argue, are stubborn, and don't forgive. *Anger makes us feel powerful.* It gives us the *illusion* that we are in control, free, and independent. But in reality, it makes us lose control.

A person who does not respect himself unconsciously concludes that others don't respect him, either. He feels that people do bad things to him purposefully, and he rarely assigns a benign motivation to their behavior. Any and every time something does not go his way causes him to deepen his anger, randomly alternating between himself and others.

To the degree we lack self-esteem, our psyche is plagued by desires, fleeting impulses, and urges that twist and pull at our thoughts. When we are alone, to quiet the unconscious voice that whispers, "I don't like me," we do whatever we can to feel good and numb the pain. We spiral downward, because a person who has a poor self-image often seeks the temporary, hollow refuge of immediate gratification and gives in to his impulses instead of rising above them.

When the ego reigns, our emotions cloud our thoughts, and our choices are unproductive and sometimes harmful. When we do not like who we are—which is true for all human beings, to varying degrees—we punish ourselves with activities that are disguised as pleasurable: excessive eating, alcohol or drug abuse, and endless, meaningless distractions. We desperately want to *love* ourselves, but instead we *lose* ourselves. Unable to invest in our own well-being, we substitute illusions for love. These ethereal pleasures mask our self-contempt, and because the comfort sought is rewarded instead by greater pain, we descend further into despair.

Everything in life is draining for the person who does not like who he has become. It's like working for a boss you despise. Even the most minor task triggers annoyance. Would you work hard for or invest in, let alone love and respect, an ungrateful and out-of-control person?

## Our Personality Is Formed

Because self-esteem and the ego are mutually exclusive, there is no such thing as a person with high self-esteem *and* an inflated ego. When our self-esteem begins to wear down, our perspective shrinks, and more of our personality comes through, filtered by our own insecurities. As a result, two distinct mentalities are produced: A person can have low self-esteem *and* a dented (though not diminished) ego—this is the doormat mentality. And one can have low self-esteem and an inflated ego—this is the arrogant person. Two people, therefore, with low self-esteem can manifest one of two different attitudes toward the same situation. The difference is that direct confrontations come from the former, while those with a dented ego are unable to voice dissatisfaction and assert themselves, so they may seek passive-aggressive ways to even the score.

These mentalities are not usually fixed. A person with low self-esteem often fluctuates between personas of inferiority (the doormat mentality) and superiority (producing arrogance), depending on the dominant personality mode at any given time. A person who is feeling inferior directs the negativity inward, manifesting hurt and sadness; a person who is feeling superior, directs the negativity outward, resulting in anger.

All of us, from time to time, vacillate between mind-sets. As an old saying goes: A person should carry two pieces of paper in his pocket, one that says, "I am nothing but dust," and the other that says, "The world was created only for my sake." The secret is knowing which piece of paper to pull out when.

This seemingly simple quote unleashes a wealth of wisdom regarding human nature. To the degree that we lack self-esteem, we react to the situation with the wrong mentality, or piece of paper. In a situation where our ego is threatened, if we have high self-esteem, we are able to perceive that we are nothing but dust. But when we suffer from low self-esteem, we erroneously believe that the world was created only for us, and we feel slighted and hurt by anyone who challenges us along the way.

---

### The Self-Esteem Test

A quick way to tell if a person has self-esteem is to observe how he treats himself and others. A person who lacks self-esteem may indulge in things for himself to satisfy only his own desire, and he will not treat others particularly well. Or he may overly cater to others because he craves their approval and respect, but not take care of his own needs. Only someone who truly has self-respect will treat both himself and others well. And when we say *well*, we do not mean he engages in short-term gratification. Rather, he invests in his long-term well-being, as well as being kind and good to others, not so they will like him, but because he likes them or because it is the right thing to do.

It's good to keep in mind that nobody likes to feel bitter and be difficult; contrary to how it may seem, this person is coming from a place of pain. While understanding how this person ticks will help us to relate more effectively to him, there are specific tactics in the following chapters that are particularly effective.

See also:

- Chapter 7: *Turn a Saboteur into Your Greatest Ally*
- Chapter 19: *The Amazing Method for Getting Along with People Who Are Emotionally Unwell*

# 10

## Quickly Handle Any Customer Complaint . . . And Turn It To Your Advantage

*"The customer doesn't expect everything will go right all the time; the big test is what you do when things go wrong."*

—Sir Colin Marshall (1933– )

The secret to swiftly—and satisfactorily—resolving a customer complaint is this: Focus more attention on the person's ego than on the actual complaint.

Customer complaints tend to fall into two general categories: (1) the customer with a legitimate grievance and a genuine reason for feeling injured and (2) the customer who's complaining about a problem that's trivial—or, at least, being blown out of proportion.

Here's what someone is *really* saying when she complains about something trivial: "I'm too important to be treated like this!" What you should realize about someone who doth protest so much is that she has a diminished sense of self-worth. That's the real reason she's so annoyed or angry.

## Strategy: The Automatic 180

No matter what kind of complaint a customer has—or which category of complainer she is—the following enhanced strategy, based on my work in mediation and customer compliance (2004), will help you quickly resolve the problem and convert the problem to an opportunity.

### Phase 1: Listen

That's right, just *listen*. Don't agree. Don't disagree. Don't argue. And even if the problem is partially the customer's fault, do not place blame. If anything other than "I'm sorry" is said to an upset customer, he'll become defensive and argumentative. The blame game is an exercise in futility, about as useful as attempting to explain proper eating and exercise habits to a man who's having a heart attack. You may think you're being helpful, but you're not. Solve the problem first. *Then* address his contribution to the problem.

Whatever you do, don't get defensive, or you're begging for an argument! Sometimes a person just needs to vent. The upside of venting is that, eventually, people run out of things to say. Don't interrupt. Just let him rant. Wait for him to run out of gas. If you interrupt, you'll only pour more fuel on the fire and give him an opportunity to find additional accusations to hurl at you.

A later chapter speaks more about building psychological rapport. Briefly, while you're listening, how you present yourself can greatly influence the attitude of the other person. If, while he's venting, your arms are crossed and your posture says, "When are you gonna stop, already?" you're heading for a confrontation. That's why simple things such as unbuttoning your coat or uncrossing your arms can make the other person feel less defensive. When you have rapport with someone, he is much more likely to feel comfortable with you.

### Phase 2: The Empathize-and-Paraphrase Two-Step

Negative emotions are always triggered by the sense that we have lost control or self-respect, and the loss may be real or imagined. So even if the person has been genuinely harmed in some way, what he finds so infuriating is that not only was he powerless to control the outcome but also someone added insult to injury by not showing him the respect he deserves. It's a double whammy—a powerful double dose of ego injury.

Your goal is to massage his ego, soothe his hurt feelings, and reempower him. Here's how.

Throughout the conversation, paraphrase what he's been saying to you, to show him that you're really listening to him and that you understand the reason for his complaint. Repeat his name couple of times (yes, it's really true; everyone loves the sound of his own name). Rebuild his ego with responses such as "If I were in your shoes, Mr. Franklin, I'd be just as upset are you are—maybe more." Or "Mr. Franklin, no one as important as you are should be treated this way." Your ability to simply listen, agree, empathize, and ego-stroke is almost certain to ease Mr. Franklin into a more agreeable frame of mind.

This simple ego reconstruction process will immediately calm him and disarm him. You've defused the bomb. You've discharged his anger and anxiety. Now you can move forward and engage him in a calm, rational dialogue.

Should you find, however, that he is still irate, here is a remarkable way to calm him down absolutely instantly: *You become enraged—but not at him, for him.* If you show your irritation or anger for how your customer was treated, you will shock him into silence every time.

---

### The Ubiquitous 80/20 Rule

The majority of businesses find that 80 percent of their regular business comes by way of 20 percent of their most loyal customers. Loyal customers are the people who do business with you on a consistent basis and who are, for all intents and purposes, customers for life. These are the people you want to hold on to. Although the 20 percent might not spend a great deal of money every time, over the years they will, statistically, account for more business than the other 80 percent.

---

### Phase 3: Ask *Him* for a Favor

You want to prove to him that you're taking his complaint seriously and send the message that you're making his problem *your* problem. You're going to ask *him* to do something for *you*.

Mr. Franklin is a guest in your hotel, and he's upset because he was waiting for an important message the day before. The message did arrive but was never delivered to him. In fact, he was repeatedly told "No messages" each time he inquired.

First, accept responsibility, and apologize. The first thing an aggrieved customer wants to hear is someone accepting responsibility. The second thing they want to hear are the two magic words, *I'm sorry.* "Mr. Franklin, the message you were waiting for was here at the desk when you came in yesterday. I'm so sorry. There really is no excuse, and I can't tell you how embarrassed I am that this happened. But I want you to know that I'll be personally responsible for your needs for the remainder of your stay. And Mr. Franklin, I was wondering if you might do me a favor. The vice president of operations is concerned about this and interested in hearing the story directly from you. Would you mind telling him yourself exactly what happened regarding your message?"

What have you just accomplished?

First, you accepted responsibility and apologized. The first thing an aggrieved customer wants to hear is someone accepting responsibility. The second thing is the magic two-word phrase, *I'm sorry*. Second, Mr. Franklin was irate because nobody cared enough to double-check whether the important message he was waiting for had arrived. Now, he feels important. Third, in asking him for a favor, you showed him that you respect him and are taking him seriously, which is what he wanted all along. In a few short minutes, Mr. Franklin evolved from feeling powerless and disrespected to thinking "Wow, they sure are making a big deal of this." Mr. Franklin believes that you care. He feels important, in control, and respected.

## Phase 4: The Bow on the Package

One final touch can wrap up the conversation on a positive note. Offer to do something special for Mr. Franklin. Tell him he'll be receiving a special surprise that you hope will compensate for your hotel's dreadful travesty of service. The surprise lets you make amends beyond a mere apology, perhaps even exceeding Mr. Franklin's expectations. Perhaps fair compensation might be a future free night's stay in one of your best suites. There's a good chance that Mr. Franklin will spend money in your hotel's restaurant and perhaps even book an extra night or two out of his own pocket.

But one caveat: Don't reveal the surprise. Let it actually *be* a surprise. Why? For three reasons: First, we all like surprises (the good kind, anyway). Second, he won't have the opportunity to say it's not good enough if he doesn't know what it is. Third, it helps him contain his anger. He won't want to risk losing the surprise, just in case it's something really good.

And guess what? Mr. Franklin will feel great about staying in your hotel the next time he's in town. You made amends, and your attentiveness to his personal needs probably has transformed him into a loyal customer.

## When It's Personal

In personal instances, where the complaint is directed at you specifically, say the following phrase and watch someone's anger dissipate before your eyes: "I couldn't be more sorry. I feel so ashamed." Again, his ego has been damaged, and he's seeking to tear you down as well as restore a sense of pride and balance. By acknowledging your own fault, you cause him to rebound. Clearly he's gotten through to you because that's exactly what he's been thinking—that you're completely in the wrong. He has nothing left to say.

See also:

- Chapter 16: *Bully-Proof Yourself and Your Office*
- Chapter 18: *Master the Art of Charisma with the Complete Psychological Formula for Instant Likability*
- Chapter 19: *The Amazing Method for Getting Along with People Who Are Emotionally Unwell*

# 11

## How to Painlessly Criticize the Highly Sensitive Employee

*"In criticism I will be bold, and as sternly, absolutely just with friend and foe. From this purpose nothing shall turn me."*

—Edgar Allan Poe (1809–1849)

One of the greatest confidence killers is when an employee feels unfairly or even fairly rebuked; particularly if he is sensitive to criticism, his mind will begin to churn with resentment and feelings of frustration and anger.

When we are hypersensitive, we are often unable to look at ourselves as the cause of the problem, because we cannot afford to be wrong emotionally. Our instincts protect our psychological well-being in much the same way as we protect our physical bodies. When our physical welfare is threatened, a natural fight-or-flight response is engaged. Similarly, when our psychological well-being is threatened, we engage our accept-or-deflect response. When a mind is healthy and strong, a challenge to the self is usually accepted and confronted directly. A mind that is not strong may instead deflect the threat. (While most people with low self-esteem will refuse to accept responsibility, those with even less self-esteem may beat themselves up and become angry and annoyed with themselves. Healthy self-esteem allows a person to recognize his mistakes, without condemning himself *or* the world.)

Just as a physically weak person will shy away from physical challenges, deflection becomes a conditioned response for the psychologically weak. A person who is emotionally unwell reacts to conflicts with "You are wrong" or "This is just how I am." There is little room for "I was wrong," the acknowledgment of personal responsibility. Such a person deflects the world and his own insecurities and, in the process, grows weaker, because the psychological self can develop only through acceptance. This is our emotional immune system. For the person who lacks self-esteem, the deflection response engages at all times. Everything is considered a threat to his psychological security.

Paradoxically, every time we refuse to acknowledge the truth about any aspect of ourselves (or condemn ourselves for being imperfect), we send ourselves the unconscious message "I am inadequate." As an analogy, today's vehicles are designed so that in an accident, the vehicle absorbs as much of the collision's energy as possible. This absorbed energy cannot be recovered, since it goes into the permanent deformation of the vehicle. In the same way, when we collide with reality and refuse to accept it, we get dented.

As life experience has shown us, once we have fully accepted something about ourselves or our lives, we no longer need to hide from it. We don't care who knows about it, or we are no longer sensitive to it. At this point, our fears of embarrassment dissolve, because there is no longer a threat of exposing ourselves. The only thing that can ever be rejected is an image. The truth, once embraced, can never be bruised or injured, yet a delusion can be shattered by a whisper or a glance.

When you deal with others, keep in mind that the *ego* is the pivotal criterion; it is the only part of us that really gets injured. Think of the ego as an image or a projection of how we would like the rest of the world to perceive us. When this image of ourselves is threatened, we become self-conscious; when it is injured, we become hurt and lash out. The ego is fragile (because it is only an image), and when you deal with others, you must seek to protect their egos if you want to spare their feelings. And the *more someone believes that what you're saying is true,* and depending on how sensitive he is to it, *the more careful you need to be.*

There's a right way and a wrong way to criticize, and how you do it can make all the difference in the world. As you may have experienced, sometimes you're open to criticism, and at other times the slightest comment can make you feel like crawling under a rock or make you extremely defensive and argumentative. *What* you say, *how* you say it, *where* you say it, and *when* you say it, all have a bearing on how your comments are received.

If you don't have to criticize this person directly, the indirect approach is always preferred. The type of relationship and the context will best determine which strategy is appropriate.

## Strategy 1: Delivering Indirect Criticism

This tactic largely eliminates the chance that your words will be taken offensively or personally. If you do it right, the person will actually feel better about himself because the very best way to give criticism is to not criticize. You can still accomplish your objective by giving praise instead.

## Phase 1: Everything's Just Fine

Tell the person you enjoy, like, and even appreciate the way he is and what he does (which is the thing you want him to change). Whether it's how he interacts with other staff members, his appearance, or how he prepares his notes, tell him that you think it's great.

## Phase 2: On Second Thought

After a short time has passed, change your mind. Let the person know that you have changed *your* mind and would like him to try something new or do something a bit different than what he has been doing. Your motivation behind the decision can be new information—for example, you just read an interesting article and were curious if the changes they suggested actually worked in increasing productivity. This way, the onus is on you; it's not about him doing something wrong, and so he will not become offended at the change request.

This removes not only him from the equation but his ego, too. Because you made the change about you and not him, it makes it hard for him feel offended.

For example, let's say that a small-business owner thinks her longtime receptionist is a bit too abrupt with clients, and she would like her to be a bit warmer and friendlier. Knowing how sensitive the receptionist is, she feels she cannot be direct in her criticism.

**Ms. Harris:** You know, Sarah, I've been meaning to tell you that I received a nice compliment for you, about how efficient you are with the clients.

**Sarah:** Thank you, Ms. Harris.

**Ms. Harris:** [later in the day] Oh, by the way, I'm expecting Mr. Mars to come by today to talk about a new product design. He may be a little uncomfortable, being that he's from out of town, so do me a favor and chat with him a little bit to make him feel extra welcome.

**Sarah:** Of course.

**Ms. Harris:** [later that day, after the client has has left] Sarah, I hope I don't drive you nuts, but it's clear to me that you really put Mr. Mars at ease. Being that you're so personable, let's try more of this chitchat stuff with the other clients and see how it goes.

You see, had Ms. Harris initially suggested that her receptionst change what she was doing, she might have been offended. But because she first reassured her that she was doing well, the change of approach has to do with Ms. Harris and not with Sarah, so it's almost impossible for her to be offended.

---

### The Eye of the Needle

A touchy subject is not necessarily something that would not only offend *him* but also offend possibly anyone you brought up the subject with. If you need to talk to him about his poor personal hygiene or his continual outbursts around the office, try this: Ask him for advice on the subject at hand. If it's not practical to inquire for yourself, tell him it's for a friend or relative. These questions open the discussion, and since you are asking him for advice, he just may turn to himself as an example.

---

## Strategy 2: Delivering Direct Criticism—Ten Steps to Constructive, Painless Criticism

Sometimes you can't beat around the bush and you need to be direct—but direct does not have to mean hurtful. When you criticize, employ as many of the 10 following psychological factors as are applicable and practical so that your rebuke is received in the way in which it is intended.

1. Without making a big deal about it, let him know you're saying this because you *care*—you care about *him* and your *relationship*.

There is an age-old saying, "Words that come from the heart enter the heart." Indeed, only sincere and heartfelt criticism has a chance of being effective. Your ability to communicate that you are motivated by genuine concern and interest for this person and your relationship with him will help your words be received in the way you intended.

2. Always criticize in private. Even if you feel that he would not mind others hearing your comments, do it behind closed doors.

3. First, emphasize her many good qualities and remarkable potential, which paves the way for a critical message to be well received. When this person truly feels that you have great respect and appreciation—perhaps even reverence or awe—then your comments will be heard in a way that does not engage the ego. For instance, "Lori, you're one of the most productive employees, and I'm continually in awe of how you do what you do. I was just wondering about . . ."

4. Criticize the *act*, not the person. In other words, instead of saying, "You're incompetent or reckless," it's better to say, "You're such a wonderful person, and this behavior doesn't seem suited to someone of your refined character."

5. Don't assume or insinuate that this behavior is something that he's doing knowingly, consciously, or deliberately. If the situation allows, approach it as something he's doing unwittingly or even unconsciously.

6. Share some of the *responsibility* if you can. Notice we don't say share the *blame*. This approach makes it you and him against this "thing," *not you against him.* You might say something like "I should have been more specific when we covered this." This approach is, of course, more effective than "I hate it when you . . ."

7. Offer the solution. If there is no answer, then you should never have brought it up in the first place, because it serves no purpose. And if you believe that no matter what you say, he will not take your advice, then it is also best not to bring it up. If you do, then you are only serving your own interests, and you will not help the situation.

8. Criticism is most effective when you tell him that he is not alone. Conveying that whatever he's done or is doing is very common (and perhaps even something that you've done yourself) diffuses the impact on the ego—meaning that he doesn't take it so personally. And that's really the reason he has become so offended.

9. The wisest man who ever lived, King Solomon, stated: "The words of the wise, when spoken gently are accepted." Remember that your tone is as important as what it is that you are saying. Speaking softly and kindly will help your message be digested in the manner you intend.

10. The best time to criticize is *when you are removed from the event.* For instance, if a supervisor wants to let Gary know that his conduct in a meeting was disturbing and inappropriate, he should not do so in that same room, let alone during the meeting.

Being removed from the environment and putting *time* between the event and your criticism are also significant. Although you may verbally assure the person that the criticism is no big deal, you don't

---

### One Simple Word

A most remarkable valuable word is *happen*. When you put this word into your sentence, it is difficult for the other person to get defensive because it downgrades your question from an answer-seeking inquiry or accusation to a mere curiosity. Note how the following sentences soften and become less confrontational with the introduction of this single word: "Did you file the report?" versus "Did you happen to file the report?" "Have you been drinking tonight?" versus "Did you happen to be drinking tonight?" "Did you correct the invoices?" versus "Did you happen to correct the invoices?"

convey that attitude by speaking up immediately. By waiting a few days, you reduce his ego attachment to the situation, and he is less sensitive to criticism. But the closer to the event (in both time and proximity) that you criticize, *the more he identifies* with his behavior, and the more defensive he will become.

See also:

- Chapter 9: *Managing Difficult People: The Psychology Behind Royal Pains*
- Chapter 17: *Sway the Room: From Jury Rooms to Board Rooms, How One Voice Can Change the Choir*
- Chapter 18: *Master the Art of Charisma with the Complete Psychological Formula for Instant Likability*
- Chapter 19: *The Amazing Method for Getting Along with People Who Are Emotionally Unwell*

# 12

## Personal Power: The Myth of Self-Discipline and the Secret to Unlimited Inspiration

*"Do we not all agree to call rapid thought and noble impulse by the name of inspiration?"*

—George Eliot (1819–1880)

t's fairly easy to look at what traits and characteristics successful people possess. Whether it's perseverance, a positive mental attitude, confidence, self-esteem, or intuition, they seem to have whatever it takes to accomplish what they want to do. To this end, the marketplace is filled with self-help books offering hundreds of techniques, ideologies, and philosophies on how to get these wonderful, magical traits that will help you stay inspired and feel impassioned.

But most people don't make it, falling back into their old habits and routines in no time. Why? Because their motivation is not powerful enough to move them into action and sustain them until they've accomplished their objective.

A flash of inspiration ignites a spark. *I can do it*, you think to yourself—finish the report, relocate offices, restructure the back office, clean up my desk—*nothing can stop me!*

But that feeling that you can do anything begins to dissipate. Your conviction wavers, and all of the reasons why it *can't* happen begin to pop up, one by one. Then, in a flood of self-doubt, it's gone. Reality sets in, robbing you of the opportunity to make good on your plan.

The flash that made you smile with knowing invincibility, the inspiration that was to change your life, has passed. Your idea is now relegated to the ranks of some other day, the land of opportunity lost. But imagine if your enthusiasm never petered out. What if you could ride above simple motivation on an unlimited stream of inspiration?

## Capturing Inspiration

Most people allow the momentum to dissipate. When the clarity fades, so does our steam; the opportunity is lost unless we take possession of it. The objective is not simply to gain an incremental movement forward; only movement in the physical world opens the next window.

Consider multileg airline travel to a remote location. If we miss one of our flights, then we lose the opportunity for the connecting flight. Regardless of whether we take action, our reality unfolds in accordance with our expectations. When we tell ourselves that our desire (enthusiasm or will power) won't last anyway, then we let the moment pass, and we prove ourselves right. The truth, however, is that we missed our next flight of inspiration by not moving in the physical world.

There is no such thing as procrastination in the universe. Each action produces a reaction, uninterrupted unless it is acted on by another force, which itself produces a reaction. Motion creates emotion; since we live in a physical world, the physical needs to be engaged while inspiration touches our soul.

It is not enough to nurture strong feelings; we can effect change only by *doing*. The purpose of creation is to unify the spiritual and the physical, elevating the latter, not to discard one form or the other.

Taking immediate swift action actually transforms that action, allowing us to accomplish much more. This is not just because we have more time but because the action is qualitatively different as a result of our moving sooner and more quickly.

When we get up early, for example, we gain more than an extra hour or two; rather, the experience of the entire day is simply different, more elevated.

Although time is linear, progress does not have to be. Times of enhanced objectivity offer us the lens through which we can view reality and realign our priorities with a more accurate sense of what is important. Hazy, illusory options are replaced by clearly lit paths. Our fears are temporarily blinded, and we have the ability to jump forward. This is how we tip the balance of free will if, and only if, we choose to take action in that defining moment.

## Sshhhh

To maximize the opportunity, remember that silence is golden. Have you ever noticed that some people who accomplish a lot seem to say very little? And the ones who are talkers just seem to do that—talk. And never really get anything done. As you move along, the less you say, the better.

There are three levels to a thought. First, you have a wonderful idea; it is infinite and expansive. You are tapped into the source of inspiration. Often we don't want to leave this dream world; many people keep plugged in for the feeling but, in doing so, don't make a reality out of their idea. There are no obstacles in a fantasy scenario, and leaving this world is scary but, of course, at the right time, necessary to move our lives forward in a meaningful direction.

Moving on to the next step, you weigh different possibilities and directions that your objective can take. Here, the thought takes form. You begin to give shape to this ephemeral, esoteric idea. But to do this, you must *constrict* it. To make it a reality, you by definition are confining the infinite to a finite world—our world. While a necessity, it is spiritually claustrophobic. Additionally, not only do you restrict the idea but also it restricts you. If you do X, then you cannot do Y.

In effect, you make it yours. You think, *I'm going to have to give up something to get something else.* At this level, you are further confined, as this is how you now see an aspect of yourself. Your self-concept is now molded around this idea—I'm a painter, I'm thin, I'm rich—*and what does all this mean?*

The next level of an idea is *speech*. Here the spiritual world blends with the physical and as such cuts us off entirely from its original source; now the idea seeks another source of fuel. For most, that becomes our own success. So we don't want to cut access too soon; it needs as much energy and momentum coming out, so that when it takes form, it has within it enough energy to carry it forward, until you recharge.

As soon as you verbalize the thought, it moves from the nonphysical world into the physical world. This second law of thermodynamics states that in any isolated system, the degree of disorder can only increase. In plain English: *Movement toward order requires energy.* So, too, an idea that is converted to an objective must be plugged into a source of energy—enough so, that it can sustain itself. Otherwise, it dies out. An objective needs structure and form to come to fruition. This requires energy. And this is why it is important to let your idea gain as much momentum as possible before it is released from your mind.

Our solution is simple. In the initial phase, don't say a word. Leave the energy within you, boiling until what comes to the surface is a result of its own forces and not because you are pushing it into the world. Keep the proverbial lid on it, and let it grow strong.

When can you talk about it? When you have already begun to make tangible progress, and you feel that no matter what anyone says, you are fully committed to moving forward.

What if you are someone who needs others' encouragement and thrives on positive feedback? Everyone appreciates words of encouragement. However, if you need accolades and others' approval, then your objective is dependent, and so are you, on the rest of the world. If you find that you must tell others, it may be a good time to reevaluate why it is you are doing what you are doing. Is this something that you want or something you think will make others like you more?

See also:

- Chapter 13: *The Five Psychological Keys to Accomplish Any Goal*

# 13

## The Five Psychological Keys to Accomplish Any Goal

*"I love deadlines. I like the whooshing sound they make as they fly by."*

—Douglas Adams (1952–2001)

While the subject of goal setting finds its way into just about every business book, this chapter crystallizes the five key psychological components involved in actualizing our objectives.

To begin with, there is no status quo in nature. The law of conservation states that organisms die if they do not grow. Moreover, just as every person is one of a kind—from their fingerprints, to their face, to their DNA—we similarly are all born with a specific purpose that is unique to us.

To obtain the highest level of fulfillment—self-actualization—we must be moving toward that which our soul desires. When we actualize our potential, we attach ourselves to the most stable force possible. Living in a way that is inconsistent or opposite to our true selves is not only unfulfilling, it is exhausting.

If we do not have a clear vision of what we want out of our lives, then we are moving through life reactively; we never realize the full force of our free will, which is to proactively move our lives in the direction of our choosing.

Too often, we confine our options to a small space, not fully recognizing the range of possibilities that extend beyond our comfort zone. Our egos lead us to believe that we are boxed in and cannot go beyond where we are, or that we can only move a little, slowly. Lack of inspiration is really lack of enthusiasm for the direction in which we believe we can move.

## Psychological Component 1: The Right Motivation

We must be honest about *why* we want what we want. So many people are miserable because they set goals based on someone else's expectations. They had every reason for doing what they did, except the right reason—because it was important to them, for their own happiness, and for creating the future they truly wanted.

If any of our objectives hinge on outside approval or acceptance, we will never be independent, and we will always look to the rest of the world for emotional reinforcement, and when we don't receive the support we need, our motivation dries up.

---

### Gold-Plated Bronze

The Olympics have three medal places: gold, silver, and bronze. This means that the fourth-place finisher is a loser. In fact, one study shows that, on average, the bronze medalist appears happier than the silver medalist. The research concludes that the athletes' emotional response is driven by comparison with the most easily imagined alternative. Silver medalists are preoccupied with having lost the gold, but bronze medalists are overjoyed to have won a medal instead of walking away with nothing (Medvec et al. 1995).

---

This idea of accomplishment—a system that is doomed to fail—is defined by an egocentric mind-set that forces us to become dependent on others to feel successful. This is sheer insanity, and a recipe for mental instability.

Even subtler, a corrupted understanding of self-esteem leads us to believe the equation: self-esteem = self-respect + self-efficacy (the ability to be effective with our choices). According to this model, we can try our very best to do what is right, but in the end, if things do not turn out as expected or hoped (i.e., if we are not effective), then we will not gain self-esteem. We may feel this to be true in our own lives. If we try to do something kind for another person but our efforts backfire and we cause the person more difficulty, then we do not necessarily walk away from the experience feeling better about ourselves.

On investigation, we find the ego lurking behind this muddled thinking. The ego is outcome-oriented. It wants results it can feel proud of and requires evidence that it is effective with a tangible, visible payoff. (When trying to motivate others, as well as ourselves, we need to be mindful that the ego must be fed. At the same time, we must remember that the higher level of inspiration comes from the knowledge that we are doing what is right, regardless of the feedback the world offers or doesn't offer.) Efficacy is achieved by the mere act of choosing to move in a meaningful direction. In other words, self-respect translates directly into self-esteem.

## A Galvanized Soul

An objective that neutralizes the ego helps us develop the flexibility that not only brings us emotional stability but also allows us to effort-lessly direct our attention. When we are engaged in this way, we can forget that we haven't eaten or slept in some time because we are divorced from the influence of the physical. Someone who can spend hours on his favorite hobby loses track of time because of his intense concentration on his objective and not on himself. Einstein's famous theory of relativity ($E = mc^2$) illustrates just this idea; as Einstein said, "When a man sits with his lover for an hour, it seems like only a min-ute. But let him sit on a hot stove for a minute and it's longer than any hour." Even though the hobby is isolating, he is not bored because he is not truly alone. When what we are doing is an act of love, we feel alive and excited and feel little or no pain.

# Psychological Component 2: A Plan of Action

Beyond choosing the direction, we also need a plan for how to get there. Not many people would go to the airport and get on a plane that takes them to just any sunny destination. We typically plan our trips by booking flights, arranging for transportation to the hotel, and perhaps even planning an itinerary so that we know exactly what we hope to accomplish. Similarly, it is irresponsible for us to have a general idea of our goals in life, without a specific plan of how to achieve them.

While many factors go into effective planning, none injures our success more than abandoning a straight path in favor of a convo-luted plan that needlessly complicates our pursuit. Occam's razor, a principle attributed to a 14th-century logician, states: "Entities should not be multiplied unnecessarily." Put more plainly, if you have two equally likely solutions to a problem, pick the simpler one. A circuitous route is based on fear of failure, fear of success, or both and is one of the ego's favorite tools. It tricks us into feeling like we are moving forward, when in actuality, we are going around in circles.

## Psychological Component 3: A Realistic Time Frame

Most people manage their lives like someone on vacation writing to a friend on a picture postcard. By the time she finishes with the introduction and usual pleasantries, she sorrowfully realizes that she has no more room left to write what she really wanted to say.

We do not run the universe, but we do run our lives. Establishing a timetable does *not* mean that we should expect specific quantifiable results, but we need a time frame in which to operate.

It is instinctive to wait until conditions become more favorable, until we have more information, or until we are in a better mood before taking an action. If we do not set a realistic schedule for our objectives (where appropriate), we are not only making a mockery of our lives but also working against the laws of human nature.

Parkinson's Law states: "Work expands to fill the time available." He expounds on this law with: "General recognition of this fact is shown in the proverbial phrase, 'It is the busiest man who has time to spare,'" and follows with this amusing anecdote:

> Thus, an elderly lady of leisure can spend the entire day in writing and dispatching a postcard to her niece at Bognor Regis. An hour will be spent finding the postcard, another in hunting for spectacles, half an hour in a search for the address, an hour and a quarter in composition, and twenty minutes in deciding whether or not to take an umbrella when going to the pillar box in the next street. The total effort that would occupy a busy man for three minutes all told may in this fashion leave another person prostrate after a day of doubt, anxiety, and toil. Granted that work (and especially paperwork) is thus elastic in its demands on time, it is manifest that there need be little or no

relationship between the work to be done and the size of the staff to which it may be assigned. A lack of real activity does not, of necessity, result in leisure. A lack of occupation is not necessarily revealed by a manifest idleness. The thing to be done swells in importance and complexity in a direct ratio with the time to be spent (Parkinson 1958).

Without a timetable, minutiae take over our lives and inflate to levels of unproductive importance.

## Psychological Component 4: Stability within Structure

When we create structure in our lives, we allow growth. Pruning, for example, is a process of directing growth—that is, energy—in the way you want it to go. Every living entity has limited resources, so cutting away and eliminating what you do not want allows greater utilization of the existing energy. Without it, our energy dissipates. Structure helps us move in a meaningful, productive direction and keeps us from succumbing to passing whims and desires.

In *The Power of Full Engagement* (2004), Jim Loehr and Tony Schwartz describe how establishing a routine is one of the most essential aspects to maximizing our energy and getting the most out of our days. Because we have only a limited amount of energy for decision making, a lack of structure and organization in our day forces us to use vital energy making countless ordinary decisions.

Imagine being let loose in a jewelry store for a five-minute shopping spree. Unless we know what we want to buy, we gravitate toward any shiny thing that catches our eye. Lack of structure does not free us; it paralyzes us.

Virtually every religion dictates a code of conduct. There are things that are permitted and things that are forbidden. Although we may agree or disagree with the specifics, such boundaries and borders are necessary to our emotional health. Someone who does not feel in control needs, most of all, a sense of structure.

Structure helps to simplify, harmonize, and synchronize our thoughts and lives. We should not simply try to fit what is important into our day; rather, we should design our day around those objectives.

When we establish our priorities, we must allocate sufficient time for them. The flip side of this rule is equally compelling. Having the courage to move in the right direction requires us to have the fortitude to close the door on what is no longer productive and constructive.

---

### More or Less

A great deal of research correlating choice and options, across many fields and industries, shows that *too many choices often paralyze a person into inaction.* One such study showed that shoppers given the option of choosing among assortments of jam showed more interest in the larger assortment (24 varieties). But when it came time to actually make a purchase, they were *10 times more likely* to buy when presented with only 6 flavors of jam, rather than 24 (Iyengar and Lepper 2000).

---

Living in contradiction to our values drains us. It forces us to justify our actions in myriad ways, but in the end, this rationalizing is draining. It creates a division within us—an emotional battle. We cannot simultaneously believe that X is all-important while spending time, energy, and effort on Y. To remain emotionally solvent, we must live, at least to some extent, in accordance with our values and what we really want in life.

People cannot completely ignore what they believe is important. Moving toward something personally meaningful—even with a single baby step—builds our emotional strength and courage.

## Psychological Component 5: Acting with Integrity

Lack of integrity saps our energy. It is like having one foot on the gas and the other on the brake. We burn out. Newton's first law of motion speaks to the tendency of a body in motion to stay in motion because of the property of inertia. What slows it down is friction; what slows *us* down is dishonesty.

We must be as truthful as possible with ourselves and others about our motivations, intentions, and actions. Whether it is keeping our word or conducting ourselves ethically, we must not think that we will gain in any way from being untruthful. The reason is simple. If your intentions or means are selfish and manipulative, not only will you *not* be successful in achieving your objective—though it may appear that you have in the short term—but you may be causing yourself harm.

Why is this so? If this is not the case—no matter how well rationalized and justified—unconscious guilt eats away at your self-esteem and causes you to be less emotionally centered and stable, leading to an array of self-destructive behaviors.

If our principles are compromised, we lose self-respect and once again become dependent and, by extension, frustrated by lack of ego-satiating, real-world progress.

The way to achieve our goals is to engage life head-on with meaningful objectives, a realistic plan for achieving them, a proper structure, and deadlines and to move forward with complete honesty and integrity.

See also:

- Chapter 12: *Personal Power: The Myth of Self-Discipline and the Secret to Unlimited Inspiration*

# 14

## How to Spot a Bluff a Mile Away: The Ultimate Bluff Buster

*"The whole world is run on bluff."*

—Marcus Garvey (1887–1940)

s an employee *really* going to leave the company if she doesn't get that raise she's demanding? Is the person on the other side of the negotiation table *really* ready to walk away, or is he bluffing? Is opposing counsel as confident about his case as he claims? How can you tell for sure?

What you're about to read is a nearly foolproof strategy for detecting every time when someone—anyone—is bluffing.

## The Confidence Game

To understand the anatomy of the bluff, you must first understand the concept of confidence. Confidence and self-esteem are often confused. Self-esteem and confidence are distinctive psychological forces, and each affects the overall psyche differently; ultimately, knowing how to distinguish between them is a critical first step in detecting a bluff.

Confidence is how effective a person feels he will be in a particular situation or within a specific realm of expertise. Self-esteem, on the other hand, is measured by how much a person likes himself and the degree to which he feels worthy of receiving good things in life. A person might feel good about himself in general (i.e., high self-esteem) yet not feel good about his odds of success in a particular situation (i.e., low confidence). And vice versa.

Consider these scenarios: A man has high self-esteem, but he's a lousy tennis player. So when he's playing a superior player, he might exhibit signs of diminished confidence, yet his sense of self-worth remains unaffected. Conversely, a senior account rep may walk into a pitch meeting with a potential client feeling confident that she can land the account, but deep down, she may not like herself much, and her situational confidence has nothing to do with her low self-esteem.

Situational confidence can be the result of several factors, for example, previous performance in a similar situation, experience and level of knowledge or expertise, feedback we've received, and how we're compared with others—both by ourselves and by others.

Now, it is true that self-esteem can have an *impact* on confidence. Studies show, for example, that the higher our overall self-esteem, the more likely we are to feel comfortable and confident when forced to perform in unfamiliar situations. The converse, however, is not true. A person who considers himself attractive, for instance, and attaches a high degree of importance to his physical appearance may very well, to the untrained eye, exhibit signs of high self-esteem.

But remember, a person's feelings of self-worth are influenced by who he is at the core, not what he possesses or what he *does*. So what you may perceive to be self-esteem is really just inflated ego—a high level of confidence with respect to his physical appearance. He may, for example, secretly believe himself to be intellectually inferior, thus unworthy of respect by his peers and unable to successfully compete on any intellectual playing field.

The key to detecting bluffing is this: The secret lies not in merely observing someone's behavior but in filtering out those signs that are intended to give the impression of self-confidence. What does a genuinely confident person look like?

We tend to assume that certain behaviors such as smiling and eye contact indicate confidence, but these gestures are easy to fake. The trick is to decipher more complex behaviors that are nearly impossible to manufacture yet easy to observe. As I explained in *You Can Read Anyone* (2007), three strategies—*perception management, direction of attention,* and *the seesaw of interest and confidence*—offer you the ability to do this.

## Strategy 1: Perception Management

Someone who is nervous but tries to appear otherwise is engaging in what's known as perception management—an attempt to present a certain image to convey the right effect. You're looking for signs that the person is trying to *appear* confident because a person who pretends to be confident is, of course, *not* confident. He's not self-assured. He's not in control of the situation. He's bluffing. And you'll catch him, once you learn to detect what a bluffer looks and sounds like.

*Sign #1: Overcompensation*

A person who is engaging in perception management generally overcompensates, and if you're looking for it, it's glaringly obvious.

Remember, the confident person isn't paying attention to his image or how he's coming across—he doesn't need to. He has genuine confidence, unlike his perception management counterpart, whose thoughts are consumed by how others are perceiving him.

---

### Cards or Guts?

In 1944, *Theory of Games and Economic Behavior*, by John von Neumann and Oskar Morgenstern, introduced the concept of game theory (a branch of applied mathematics), the objective of which is to mathematically predict behavior in a wide range of strategic situations. It offers two possible motives for bluffing: "The first is to give an (false) impression of strength in (real) weakness; the second is to desire to give a (false) impression of weakness in (real) strength." A poker player bets heavily, keeps raising the pot. Has he got the cards or just the guts to bluff? If he's bluffing, he wants to show that he's not timid, so he might bet quickly, toss in his money quickly. But suppose he does have a good hand? What will he do? That's right, he'll deliberate a bit, playing his chips slowly and cautiously to suggest that he isn't so sure about his hand.

---

When people pretend to be confident, whether betting a poker hand or negotiating a corporate buyout bid, they manipulate how confident they appear. In other words, they try to create an impression that's the opposite of how they actually feel. The bluffer bets quickly. The confident guy with the good hand waits a moment or two, pretends to be deliberating. Each of these players' behaviors is exactly the opposite of how confident they actually feel.

And you can count on this to be true for almost every situation in both your work life and personal life. If a person reacts too quickly and seemingly confidently, he may be trying too hard to prove that he's confident, which almost invariably means he really isn't.

A confident person does not need to tell people he's confident. Someone who pretends to be sure of himself, or of anything, for that matter, makes gestures that are consistent with a confident attitude but often goes a little overboard. Look for *overcompensation.*

---

### Telltale Eye Language

The eyes speak louder than words. Little or no direct eye contact is a classic sign of deception. A person who is lying to you will ferociously attempt to avoid making eye contact with you because he has a subconscious fear that you can see through him, that his eyes are a window into his soul. Perhaps he feels guilty about lying and can't face you, so his eyes dart from side to side, or he glances down at the floor. But when we're telling the truth, especially when we're being falsely accused of something, we tend to focus completely on our accuser—our concentration is fixed. We lock eyes with him, as if to pin him in place until we can convince him we're telling the truth.

---

Law enforcement knows that a person who is lying often displays deliberative, pensive behaviors such as stroking or tapping his chin, as if he is giving serious thought to a question he's just been asked, even though he knows the answer, of course. But his display is intended to conceal the true answer.

Another clue that a person is overcompensating and trying to manage the impression you have of her is when she tries to regain the psychological advantage for no good reason.

For example, a supervisor is breaking the news to James that she chose someone else instead of him to represent their department on a special company task force: "I know you were hoping to be on the task force, James, but Richard has the right experience. It's not personal." If James is bluffing, he might say: "Oh, I've got a lot on my plate these days, anyway." Maybe he's disappointed because he was really counting on being chosen for the task force, but he works very hard to conceal his disappointment, save face, and regain the psychological advantage. If he simply replied, "Sure, I understand," or something to that effect, it's a sign that he's not interested in the promotion and has no need to manipulate her perception of him.

### Sign #2: Superfluous Gestures

In a serious situation, any gesture that's superfluous is a sign that someone is trying to seem calm and confident. Often, these cues may be nonverbal. For instance, the subject of a police interrogation may yawn, as if to show that he is relaxed and calm, perhaps even bored. A person who is seated may slouch or stretch her arms to cover more territory, as if to prove how comfortable she is. Or the subject may busy himself picking lint off his shirt, suggesting that he's preoccupied with something else and that the matter at hand is so trivial that, clearly, he is not worried.

The problem is that someone who's innocent and being wrongly accused would be quite indignant and hardly focusing on something as trivial as lint on his shirt.

Another example: A detective is questioning the parents of a girl who appears to have been kidnapped. At one point, the father remarks to the detective that his daughter may already be dead. Shortly afterward, the detective hands him a cup of coffee. Suppose the father says something casual like: "Thank you so much. I can really use the caffeine on a day like this." He's engaging in perception management, trying to convey that he's a polite, considerate, and well-mannered person, and something is likely to be very wrong with his story.

Another type of superfluous behavior is trying to look the part. A person who alters his appearance so that he conveys a particular image with no good reason for it doesn't really *feel* what he's portraying. His inner self does not match his outer self. For example, a commercial real estate agent meets a potential buyer on a Saturday afternoon to show a new office building. The agent is dressed to the nines—suit and tie on a Saturday afternoon. And when the client arrives, he's on his cell phone in the midst of an important call. What can you assume? He is not a prosperous Realtor.

---

### Physical Factors

Always look for physical signs of nervousness. When someone is nervous, swallowing becomes difficult, so be on the lookout for the hard swallow, the person who is literally all choked up. Throat clearing is also famously a sign of nervousness. You'll notice that public speakers often clear their throats before speaking. Why? They're nervous. Anxiety causes excess mucus to form in the throat. Also look for vocal changes. Vocal cords tighten when a person is stressed, which produces a higher octave or different pitch.

---

### Strategy 2: Direction of Attention

Imagine an athlete or musician who delivers a flawless performance. He's not focused on himself, his appearance, or his performance. A pro basketball player, for instance, who's about to shoot the ball has only the intention of making a goal. All other potential distractions are drowned out. He's in the zone. He merely executes his intention without focusing on himself. He's not self-aware or self-conscious. If he became self-conscious, he would become hyperaware—distracted from the primary task at hand—and his attention and focus would be divided among himself, his surroundings, and others.

A confident person is able to focus on the primary objective, and the *I* disappears. A nervous person has an ego consuming her thoughts, and she can't help focusing on herself, her fear, and her anxieties. She's literally self-aware of every little thing she says and does. What were once unconscious actions—for example, what her hands are doing or how she's posed in a chair—become part of her heightened state of awareness, and her actions appear more awkward.

Whether it's a meeting, a date, or an interrogation, a confident, in-control person can reach for ordinary objects such as cigarettes, pens, or elevator buttons without paying attention to either his hand or the object. The insecure person, by contrast, doesn't feel competent to do other things while conversing, so his eyes may monitor his own movements.

Let's look at the psychological mechanics behind competence: Competency has four levels. Unconscious incompetence is a state in which a person is unaware that he is not performing correctly. Conscious incompetence is awareness that one has not acquired the skill set necessary to be as effective and successful as he would like to be. Conscious competence is when a person has heightened awareness; he knows and understands what he needs to do to succeed, and he will generally succeed as long as he follows the system he's learned. Unconscious competence is when a person can perform competently—without his full or even partial attention—instinctively and automatically.

These four levels of competence are analogous to learning to drive a stick shift. A task that starts out completely foreign and unfamiliar eventually evolves to a level of skill or competency at which the driver can shifts gears unconsciously. He does not need to consciously focus on what he's doing.

With respect to detecting bluffing, the second, third, and fourth levels of competence give us insight into a person's confidence levels. (The first level is irrelevant because the person is not even aware of what he needs to do to be effective—let alone be confident that he can perform effectively.)

Let's say that an employee has just informed you that she will leave the company unless she gets a $5,000 raise within the next two weeks. As she speaks, you notice she reaches for a can of soda easily within her grasp. But she watches her hand extend to the drink and then watches her hand as it brings the can to her lips. You can bet that she's nervous and unsure of herself. She does not even trust her ability to do what she has done thousands of times before—sip a drink—without paying careful attention. What should be a matter of unconscious competence slips down a notch to conscious competence—a heightened level of awareness.

If you know what to look for, confidence (or the lack thereof) is easy to detect. Simply observe whether the person is focused on himself and what his hands and body are doing.

## Strategy 3: The Seesaw of Confidence and Interest

Another great way to detect a bluffer is to ruffle his feathers a little and see how he responds. Here's how it works: A person's confidence is directly proportional to his interest level. The most confident woman in the world may suddenly find herself smitten with insecurity and lack of confidence in the presence of a man she's attracted to and wants to impress. And a man who has been unemployed for years will, upon landing a good interview, have far less confidence than a candidate who is gainfully employed but seeking a new job. Indeed, once the interview is over, the insecure unemployed man will replay the entire interview again and again in his mind. He will obsess over his answers to the interviewer's questions. Did he say enough? Or did he say too much? He will be consumed by his fear that he won't get the job. Why is he obsessing? Because his options are limited.

By artificially shifting a person's ability to gain what he wants, you can alter his perception of the situation and reveal his true degree of interest. Therefore, offer information that leads him to believe his odds of getting what he wants are decreased. If he becomes annoyed or frustrated, he's clearly interested and may have been trying to play it cool. But if he doesn't seem bothered that his odds have dwindled, he's not so interested, extremely confident, and not bluffing.

See also:

- Chapter 5: *The Foolproof Strategy to Keep Any Employee from Stealing*
- Chapter 7: *Turn a Saboteur into Your Greatest Ally*

# 15

## Find Out If Your Employees Are Doing Drugs or Drinking on the Job with a 30–Second Nonaccusatory Conversation

*"Drugs have taught an entire generation of Americans the metric system."*

—P. J. O'Rourke (1947– )

f you suspect that an employee is abusing substances, research suggests 12 behavioral red flags that you want to watch out for. While all of these traits may not automatically mean drug abuse or addiction, the more of these signs that show, the more likely that there is indeed a problem.

---

### All Too Common

Drug addiction is more common than most people think. According to a national survey on drug use and health conducted in 2003, 7.8 percent of employees polled admitted to illicit drug use in the past month, and 1.9 percent had been either dependent on or abusing drugs for the past year. The abuse was higher among employees who were 18 to 25 years old and declined for people beyond that age.

---

1. If an employee is absent a great deal and, in particular, if the absences occur with little or no prior notification, this can signal a problem. If an employee overuses sick days or mental health days, then you need to have a talk.

2. If an employee disappears from work frequently, whether it is for 10 to 15 minutes or for longer spans of time, this is a concern. Also, if an employee often takes long breaks or lunches, then it is time to look deeper. In particular, if the employee gets defensive when asked about the absences or gives excuses that don't make sense, you need to find out what lies beneath.

3. If an employee is not dependable and reliable, such as not meeting deadlines or keeping appointments, this could signal trouble.

4. If an employee's work performance has plenty of up and down cycles and goes from high productivity to low productivity for no obvious reason, then this is not a good sign.

5. Mistakes made on a regular basis caused by bad judgment, poor decision making, lack of focus, or inattention need to be looked into further.

6. Memory loss, confusion, and difficulty in concentrating on tasks, following instructions, and paying attention to details can signal that the employee is having a problem.

7. If a work task that an employee previously had done with ease suddenly takes more time and more effort, then the employer needs to address the issue.

8. Interpersonal relations can break down between coworkers if one of them has developed a problem with drugs or alcohol.

9. If an employee comes to work looking dirty or disheveled and seems to not care about appearance or personal hygiene, then a problem has arisen.

10. An employee who rarely if ever admits to mistakes at work or refuses to admit to slip-ups or oversights could be harboring a problem such as substance abuse.

11. Personality changes to varying extents can be a clear-cut sign of problems such as mood swings, anxiety, and depression; a lack of impulse control; and suicidal thoughts and/or threats.

12. Long sleeves when the weather is very hot is a suspicious sign.

Employees who isolate themselves personally and professionally are probably in a precarious situation.

## Strategy 1: Let Me Ask Your Advice

Got a suspicion that an employee is drinking on the job or abusing drugs? Unless you catch him red-handed, making an accusation can be prickly territory. If you're wrong, you run the risk of damaging the supervisor-employee relationship and may even trigger unpleasant legal repercussions.

A technique I introduced in *Never Be Lied to Again* (1998) is a great way to find out if your employee is up to something, without making a single accusation. The psychology behind these strategies has since been instituted in a variety of corporate security programs, as well as by local and federal law enforcement agencies. Here's how it works.

Ask your employee's advice on how to solve the problem you suspect him of creating. For example, you might say, "Paul, I wonder if you could help me with something. It's come to my attention that someone in the warehouse has been smoking marijuana during breaks. How do you think we should go about clearing this up?"

If he's innocent, he's going to offer some advice and be flattered that you respected him enough to ask his opinion. If he's guilty, he'll seem uncomfortable and may try to assure you that *he'd* never do anything like that. Either way, you've opened the door to deeper probing.

Here's a twist on this technique that can reveal great insight into the person's innocence or guilt. Broach the subject but in a nonchalant, off-the-cuff way, as if you're just sort of thinking out loud. For example, you might say, "Isn't it amazing that employees have the nerve to do drugs and not worry about whether security cameras in the hallways are recording them?" or "Isn't it amazing that employees do drugs on the job and don't worry about whether someone will report them?"

You may get all kinds of answers in response, and it can be difficult to decipher which ones stem from worry and which from curiosity. Therefore, quickly *change the subject.* Then observe what happens next. Does the employee suddenly seem happier or more relaxed? Observe his posture. Does it become more relaxed and less defensive? The telltale indicator of guilt is a sudden mood change that indicates discomfort with the previous subject matter. He may even smile or laugh nervously.

Test him to see if he tries to change the subject at the first opportunity. Find a good place to pause, and wait to see if he leaps at the opportunity to switch topics. In a nutshell: *The guilty wants to end the conversation; the innocent wants to extend it.*

## Strategy 2: Shifting Time—the Power of Recession

This technique produces truly remarkable results by combining a sequence of psychological principles.

Let's say, for example, that your wife calls you at work and informs you that your 15-year-old daughter sneaked the family car for a joy ride and was just escorted home by police officers. You'd probably be upset, wouldn't you? Now, let's change one element of this saga: Your wife tells you that your 15-year-old daughter sneaked the family car for a joy ride and was escorted home by the police, except that your wife doesn't tell you the story until 10 years after it happened. Your daughter is now 25. Your reaction is likely to be considerably milder, isn't it? In fact, admit it: You'll probably laugh. Why? Because time has passed.

Now, let's look at this example from your daughter's perspective. If your daughter borrowed the car without permission 10 years ago, she would probably feel that she could mention it with full immunity. She certainly doesn't have to worry about being punished now, and she probably figures you'd find it amusing at this point. It's doubtful, though, that she would have felt quite so comfortable confessing her deed 10 years ago, the day she actually swiped the car.

No doubt you've heard that time heals all wounds. It's true that time is a powerful psychological influence that can shift our perspective dramatically. Event timelines have two fundamental points: (1) the date the event occurred and (2) the date you became aware of the event. Once either factor has receded into the past, the event is no longer timely and perhaps seems irrelevant, and this aging effect greatly reduces the perceived significance of the event.

Let's say you're a supervisor at a food brokerage company. You suspect several nightshift warehouse workers of drinking on the job. Hold a conversation with one of the suspected employees in which you casually let the conversation turn to drinking, and say: "Oh, I knew all along that you guys were drinking on breaks." Suggest that it's not such a big deal, but add: "You had to know I knew. How else do you think you could have gotten away with it for so long? I hope you don't think I'm a complete fool." (The "complete fool" phrase is doubly powerful because the employee won't want to risk offending you, on top of everything else.) Next, you say something that suggests that you understand how he could have gotten caught up in purloining food [drinking when everybody else was doing it]. "I know it was just a few little items here and there [just took a couple of nips here and there]. And that you were just going along with it because you were scared of what the others would do. It's really okay. I know you're not that kind of person."

See how nicely this works? Confessing will make him feel that he's a good person, the kind of person his boss thinks he is. He's living up to your expectations. Plus, because he assumes that you've been aware for some time and there have thus far been no repercussions, he has no reason to believe that his job is in jeopardy.

Contrast this response with what happens if your approach indicates that you just found out. In that case, he won't know how you're going to respond or what negative result may potentially follow. By shifting when you first became aware of the event into the past, he has no reason to believe that your relationship—and his job—won't continue to be business as usual.

## Strategy 3: You and Me against the World

This sequence of psychological tactics is powerful, but the setup requires the cooperation of a third party. The key is to enlist a friend or coworker to make the accusation for you. For example, "Mel, I was talking to Cindy, and she told me she's getting pretty tired of you being stoned on the job."

Notice that part of the beauty of this technique is that it removes practically all doubt that *you're* being deceptive; you retain maximum credibility. And your accomplice is thoroughly believable because people rarely suspect a third-party arrangement. See, at this point, Mel will only be concerned about Cindy's disapproval of his actions.

Suppose he still won't confess? Switch the focus. Say, "Are you kidding? It's common knowledge." Then dangle the bait, "But I think I know how you can smooth things over with her." If he takes the bait, he's guilty. After all, an innocent person wouldn't need to smooth things over with someone for something he hasn't done.

Still not getting the answer you're looking for? Your accomplice should say something like "Okay. But are you *sure*?" Any sign of hesitation is likely to be a sign of guilt because he's buying time to weigh his options.

See also:

- Chapter 14: *How to Spot a Bluff a Mile Away: The Ultimate Bluff Buster*

# 16

## Bully-Proof Yourself and Your Office

*"When a resolute young fellow steps up to the great bully, the world, and takes him boldly by the beard, he is often surprised to find it comes off in his hand, and that it was only tied on to scare away the timid adventurers."*
—Ralph Waldo Emerson (1803–1882)

Workplace bullying is a frequent contributor to employee leavings. In August 2007, Zogby International conducted 7,740 interviews in conjunction with Workplace Bullying Institute. Key findings from the WBI-Zogby survey include:

- Thirty-seven percent of workers have been bullied.
- Most bullies are bosses (72 percent).
- Most targets (57 percent) are women.
- Bullying is four times more prevalent than illegal harassment.
- Sixty-two percent of employers ignore the problem.
- Forty-five percent of targets suffer stress-related health problems.
- Forty percent of bullied individuals never tell their employers.

The survey results clearly show that bullying tolerance is expensive for employers. Tangible costs include turnover costs such as recruitment, interviewing, and hiring; absenteeism and lost productivity; workers' compensation; and both short- and long-term disability insurance. Intangible costs include employee sabotage and difficult long-term recruitment and retention due to a tarnished reputation.

Bullies, then, need to be put in their place. From a management perspective, training programs to help employees recognize and report such behavior is imperative. From a personal standpoint—you can have a little more fun.

## The Argument Bully: Mastering the Art of Verbal Self-Defense

Ever find yourself in the middle of a ridiculous argument, only to realize that you don't care about the issue at hand and can't even remember how you got trapped in this argument in the first place? Having advanced verbal self-defense skills can be a valuable asset.

Much has been written about the art of effective arguing. Some believe that verbal self-defense means fighting back, that you must annihilate your opponent in order to win the argument. For this, you'll need a steady stream of hostile, barbed rejoinders that you can whip out at a moment's notice. Others suggest that you take a deep breath and tell him that you respect his feelings, et cetera, et cetera.

These strategies almost never work, especially when you're dealing with someone who wants—in one way or another—to cause you harm. If your opponent was interested in a calm, intelligent exchange of ideas, you wouldn't be deadlocked in argument in the first place.

The powerful psychological tactics we're about to reveal assume that you've got a bully on your hands and that the rational communication pipeline has been shut down. You'll learn how to fend off your bully and take control of the situation.

When someone is attacking you, your natural instinct is to jump in and defend yourself. But it's the most common—and biggest—mistake you can make. The argument bully may pepper you with silly questions that have no intelligent answer.

Each of our strategies takes into account the first rule for handling a verbal bully: *Never, ever, get defensive.* The second you start defending yourself against an accusation, you've lost. And you'll be slogging uphill from then on. Defending yourself only lends credence to your bully's accusation. Ever watched someone get defensive? Not only does he *appear* guilty, he quickly becomes a verbal punching bag. Once you get defensive, you *stay* defensive. Remember, you can't win with your back against the wall.

### Strategy 1: Verbal Kung Fu

A quick and precise way to fend off a verbal assault is to simply reject the premise. For instance, your boss accuses you of not putting your heart into your work lately. The premise is that you don't work very hard or at least you don't work as hard as your boss thinks you should. You don't want to argue from that point because then, no matter what you say, no matter how vigorously you protest that you give 110 percent every single day, you'll still be defending yourself and thus already operating from a disadvantage.

Even if you can point out that you work longer hours than anyone else in your department, your boss can always say, "You might work hard, but you don't work smart" or "Your problem is you're not good at delegating." Now you've opened the door for a further itemization of what your problems are, and you have even more vague accusations to defend against. Now you're officially engaged in an argument, one that's difficult to win.

The following tactical maneuvers will show you how to handle situations like these, turn any argument to your advantage, and head off the verbal bully at the pass.

Because your objective is to not get defensive, you must, of course, immediately go on the offensive. The beauty of this approach is that it allows you to defend yourself *without being defensive.*

When you're asked a question that you feel is a cheap shot (for example, "You're not putting your heart into your work lately"), respond with "What answer would satisfy you?" You'll receive one of two kinds of responses. If you get an "I don't know," respond with "Well, if you don't know what the answer is supposed to be, how am *I* supposed to know?" His other possible response—the likelier response—will be something more specific. But that's okay. At least now you've got something to work with. And incidentally, note that *he's* the one answering questions now, not you. He's the one with his back against the wall.

For instance, a coworker says: "You don't have enough experience to be running this department." Instead of saying, "Yes, I do because ..." (which is defensive, because now your opponent can pick apart your reasons), your answer should be "How many years experience do you think I should have?" For argument's sake, let's say that she says, "At least ten years." You then reply, "Well, what about nine, is that too few?" *Now she has to defend her answer, as opposed to your having to defend yours!*

And here's the best part: When you ask her to be more specific, it becomes much harder for her to justify her beliefs. For example, she now has to explain the difference between the 10 years and 9 years. (No one can do this!) And even if she does provide a justification for her position, you simply continue to press her further as to *why* she feels this way; keep asking her to be *more specific.* Specificity always gets people in trouble.

Your strategy, in a nutshell, is to *get her to explain why her premise is right, as opposed to your having to explain why your answer is right*. In the legal arena, this tactic is known as reframing the argument. And imagine how she'll sound to anyone who overhears the conversation. She'll appear to be rigid, unyielding, and argumentative because she's now in the position of having to defend herself against her own ideas.

Part of the secret to this technique's effectiveness is that there's something she won't realize in advance: Any general belief that is reduced to specifics almost always seems silly when you begin to defend it.

## Strategy 2: Refusing Ownership

When someone is rude to us, it upsets us, and our natural reaction is to protect our ego. We're likely respond with something like "How dare you talk to me like that! I didn't do anything wrong!" But when you do that, you're making this angry person your problem.

Why let someone else dictate how you feel? When you allow yourself to get angry, you've just given someone else control over your emotional state. And that's a lot of power to give away, especially to someone who disrespects you enough to be rude to you.

If you simply resist that initial inclination to get defensive, you'll be surprised at how much power you've just gained over your bully. Don't take ownership of his problem. It's *his* problem, not yours. So, for instance, instead of responding "How dare you talk to me like that!" defuse the bomb with a response such as "You seem to be having a rough day" or "You seem upset."

The second you respond with a statement that includes the pronouns *I* or *me*, you dramatically alter the psychological dynamic. You've created a partnership between *you* and *him*, whereas if you use only the pronoun *you*, the problem remains his sole property. And you've left the ball in his court.

And something else: You'll find that when you don't respond defensively, you won't become nearly as upset by the whole exchange. You'll realize that it has nothing to do with you, as long as you don't assume ownership.

## Strategy 3: The Little Package of Advice

Sometimes bullying is disguised in the form of a little unwanted advice package. We've all received these, at one time or another. Just offer a sincere thanks to the person for her insights and move on, even if the remark strikes you as unproductive or self-serving. You can open your little package later and decide whether it contains any useful advice. It just might, but for you to accept constructive advice, you may need to take a little breather to separate the message from the messenger.

If the advice is more *de*structive than *con*structive, recognize that she may be coming from a place of pain and that she needs to attack you in order to feel good about herself. If you get angry, annoyed, and defensive, it's essentially the same as kicking the shins of a 90-year-old man who picks a fight with you. You can't win. Try to have compassion and empathy for her—regardless of what you suspect her motives to be. And rise above it. "Thank you, I'll give that some thought" can back down a bully in no time flat.

Now, you might consider adding one final touch to your response: Ask her how she became so capable in or knowledgeable about whatever arena she's dispensing advice in. Remember, this tactic works only if you can refrain from being sarcastic! Consider these examples:

> **Comment:** Mary, you know that speech you made yesterday really didn't go over too well.
>
> **Your Response:** Really? Thanks for letting me know. A lot of people wouldn't tell me that because they'd think I'd get upset. Where did you learn so much about public speaking?
>
> **Comment:** You know, Aaron, I could have told you that your turnaround projections wouldn't convince anybody.
>
> **Your Response:** Really? I really appreciate you looking out for me. How would you have handled it?
>
> **Comment:** I thought you were trying to lose weight. Should you be eating that?
>
> **Your Response:** Oh, you're so sweet for reminding me that I'm dieting. Thank you. You seem to have such great willpower. I wish you'd tell me your secret!

Always keep in mind that a person who is disrespectful to you disrespects herself. She craves respect. Give it to her. When you thank her and ask her advice, you not only end her attack but also feed her psyche and satisfy that craving. In fairness, just because she didn't deliver her criticism in a caring way does not necessarily mean she doesn't care about you. She simply may not possess the skills to critique you with kindness and diplomacy.

## Strategy 4: Refocus the Dialogue

Okay, but suppose you're losing the argument, the facts are simply not on your side, and you just want out? Don't worry; this exit strategy will rescue you.

If you don't like the question you're being asked, don't answer it. *Answer a different question.* Simply reply with something like: "In terms of what?" or "How exactly do you mean?" This forces the person to rephrase the question, which means you can now answer this new, more precise question instead of the original one—all without seeming to have dodged answering the question!

For instance, you're asked, "How come all the employees are complaining about the new shift rules?" Well, there's no way you can win by answering that. It's like asking a man if he's still beating his wife. Any answer is a bad one. So ask your questioner to clarify her question, and then answer the *new specific question*. Here's how the exchange might go:

> How come all the employees are complaining about the new commission plan?
>
> How exactly do you mean?
>
> Oh, Jan and Thom have complained that the new top tier bonus isn't enough.

Now you've got *two people* complaining specifically about the top tier bonus instead of every worker complaining about the entire commission plan. It's just become an easier situation to manage. But you want to narrow the question even further. Why? So the questioner will begin to seem argumentative, not you.

"Top tier bonus?" you reply, adding, "What percentage do they think they should get?" You can see that the wind beneath her argument will now begin to dissipate rather quickly.

Think about what you've just accomplished. You've managed to answer a new question, put her on the defensive, and force her to get specific, which, as we saw earlier, sets the stage for her to ultimately look silly and seem argumentative. Who won?

But remember, you want to avoid appearing as if you're trying to dodge the question. Dodgers lose credibility and seem uncooperative and argumentative, which only sets you up for more argument.

If this approach isn't suitable, here's another way to gently shift the focus without being argumentative and enable a more constructive, useful conversation—again, all without being defensive.

When you're asked a tough question, respond with "I think what you're really saying is …" (and then change the question).

Say you're told, "I don't think you're ready for this promotion." Respond with "I think what you're really saying is that if I could show you how I can not only reduce costs by 50 percent but also increase revenue by 30 to 40 percent, I'd be 'ready,' right?" Now that wasn't his question at all, of course. But your answer addresses the motivation behind the question. And most important, *he is forced to agree with you*, simply because if you can do what your answer implies you can, there should be no other reason why you wouldn't deserve the promotion, right? Next, you lay out your strategy for increasing revenue and cutting costs, and you never look back.

You're told, "You don't seem to have much respect for your colleagues." You say, "I think what you're really saying is that you've been hurt and I need to prove to you that it will never happen again." Now you have something specific to work with.

Let's look at one more example. You're asked, "How could you have created such a serious problem?" You reply, "If I understand you correctly, I think what you really want to know is what other factors were involved that you may not be aware of?" That's not his question, but it's a much easier one to answer because you're also implying that the debacle was not—or at least not entirely—your fault. It gives you an opportunity to address specific issues that contributed to the problem.

It's practically impossible to answer an abstract question intelligently. Refocus the question to something clear and specific, and *then* respond. Don't let anyone goad you into answering a vague question or remark. You can't win. Change the question, reduce it to specifics, and then answer.

## Strategy 5: Handling the Stealth Bully—Two Great Techniques

What do you do when the bullying comes in the form of passive-aggressive attitudes and behavior? First, what exactly is passive-aggressive behavior? For our purposes here, it describes a person who does not choose to confront situations or conflicts directly and head-on. Rather, she gets back at the person indirectly by causing harm or inconvenience in a seemingly innocent manner. For instance, if your assistant feels that you don't give her the respect she wants, even though she is bothered, she feels unable to speak with you directly about it. Therefore, she, partly unconsciously, may misplace files, come in late, or not return important calls as a way of settling the score.

She is unable to confront you and the situation head-on, so she chooses to back down, only to get back at you in another way, at another time, whether it is by being late, seemingly forgetting to do something important, or just generally inconveniencing you.

### *Technique 1: Make You Both Look Good*

Ask for the person's help on the very thing he is making difficult for you. The psychology behind this technique is twofold. First, he makes an investment, but he also wants his investment to pay off, which can happen only if things go easy for you. If he makes life more difficult, the stress and turmoil may cause you to be ineffective—and his advice becomes useless. We all want to be right, and so he will try to make things as easy as possible for you so that you can benefit from his wisdom.

For example, an office manager has a secretary, Marge, who frequently misfiles things. Chloe could ask Marge to devise an improved system for filing. Once it is in place, the only way Marge's system can be useful is if Chloe does not spend her time trying to track down files. Therefore, Marge will not only refrain from sabotage but also try to make things easier on Chloe. The less time Chloe spends looking for files, the more effective Marge's system is.

### *Technique 2: I Understand*

This technique makes it impractical for someone to act passive-aggressively toward you. First, you bring his behavior into the open by telling him that you are aware of what he has been doing. Next, you tell him that you know why he has been doing what he has and that you completely understand. The twist here is to make your thinking based on a problem other than his passive-aggressive behavior.

For example, Hillary has a coworker, Wally, who keeps forgetting to give her phone messages in a timely way. She tells him, with a very casual, nonaccusatory tone, "Wally, I understand why you forget to give me my messages sometimes. It's because the workload is just too much for you, and you get a little overwhelmed. I want you to know that I don't take it personally, whatsoever. You can't help yourself, even if you want to."

Wally, of course, denies the behavior, his motivation, or both. Hillary then follows up, saying, "I'm sorry. Maybe I shouldn't have said anything." Now whenever a situation comes up, if Wally doesn't give Hillary her phone messages, he will be admitting that she was right—and his ego won't let him do this.

We should remind ourselves that the harder the outside, the softer the inside. It is nature's way of protecting what is vulnerable. So if you want to understand some of the core issues (as well as gain some additional techniques), check the related chapters.

See also:

- Chapter 7: *Turn a Saboteur into Your Greatest Ally*
- Chapter 18: *Master the Art of Charisma with the Complete Psychological Formula for Instant Likability*
- Chapter 19: *The Amazing Method for Getting Along with People Who Are Emotionally Unwell*
- Chapter 20: *Instantly Resolve Any Personality Conflict*

# 17

## Sway the Room: From Jury Rooms to Board Rooms, How One Voice Can Change the Choir

*"In the modern world of business, it is useless to be a creative original thinker unless you can also sell what you create. Management cannot be expected to recognize a good idea unless it is presented to them by a good salesman."*

—David M. Ogilvy (1911–1999)

Have you ever been in a meeting where one person completely wows everyone? It's almost as if he put the people in the room into some sort of trance. Odds are that he employed at least some of the following techniques that give one person the ability to sway the thinking of others.

## Strategy 1: The Vocal Majority

It is often thought that by swaying those with a sphere of influence, we create a trickle-down effect that helps to move the common folk to our way of thinking. So we spend our time, energy, and resources trying to win over these elite few, with the hope and expectation that their stature and standing will cause others to follow. In theory, it makes sense, and in reality, it does work.

However, studies show that when someone, even a person who is known to be uninformed—or worse, apathetic—changes his thinking, others are likely to reconsider their positions, and some are likely to follow suit. Although there is no precise way to measure the impact in every situation, there are certainly times when we will get more bang for our buck by going after the little guy.

---

### The Asch Experiment

In this classic experiment, subjects were asked to find the best match for the line in Exhibit 1 from the lines in Exhibit 2 (see Figure 17.1). When asked alone, almost every person judged line A as the correct match. When the subject first listened to several people who were in on the experiment and who unanimously gave a wrong answer, however, *76 percent* of the subjects responded, at least once, in accord with the group, rather than

---

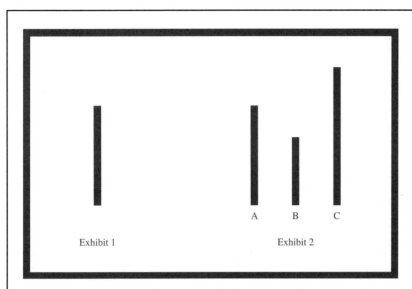

Exhibit 1                                    Exhibit 2

trusting their own judgment and their own objective, clear-cut answer. There was no pressure to conform, only the subtle influence of the others.

Can't find even one ally, you say? You can be your own sphere of influence and sway others all by yourself! New research reveals even if only one member of a group expresses an opinion, *others are likely to see it as representative of the whole group.* A study published recently in the *Journal of Personality and Social Psychology* examined exactly this situation to test how people judge the distribution of opinion.

The experiment, carried out by Kimberlee Weaver and colleagues (2007), found that if one person in a group repeats the same opinion *three times,* it has 90 percent of the effect of three different people in that group expressing the same opinion.

The authors extrapolate that it comes down to *memory;* because repetition increases the accessibility of an opinion, we assume it has a higher prevalence. Experiments of memory and attitude and behavior conclude that people often base their self-concept on availability, or how easily they can bring information to mind. For instance, if you were asked to think of several times when you acted ambitiously and were able to recall these events with relative ease, then you would think of yourself as ambitious. Conversely, if you could not come up with an example, then you would conclude that you were cautious and conservative.

Of course, we can say, for example, that a person cannot come up with such examples because this is the way he is. However, findings indicate that even when these memories are few and far between, as in the case of the person who is not ambitious, if he rehearses recalling these memories so they are easily brought to mind, he will then see himself as more ambitious.

To employ this tactic, find different ways to communicate the same idea so that you don't sound like a broken record, just a familiar opinion that reinforces the same important message.

---

### Men Are from Mars

Because men are essentially egos with legs and women are relationship-oriented, the sexes respond differently to persuasion attempts via e-mail. Men are more easily swayed by e-mail because it sidesteps their competitive tendencies. Women, however, are much less susceptible to e-mail and more flexible and accommodating in face-to-face encounters (Guadagno and Cialdini 2002).

---

The fact remains that conformity and social pressure are strongest when people do not have personal allies, others in their corner, agreeing with them. So don't let them gain confidence in their numbers. Speak and sway individually wherever you feel that the group may unite against your desired direction.

## Strategy 2: Fair and Flexible

There are always those who present a stronger front than reflects their true feelings, and confidence in your ideas will propel them toward your position. Confidence is most easily expressed in consistency, which is why your passionate and unwavering belief will inspire these people, and others, to rethink and reevaluate the situation, even without the introduction of any new information. If you waffle, hedge your bets, or show signs of giving in or changing your mind, your ability to sway is greatly reduced.

At the same time, you also want to avoid appearing rigid and unreasonable. Studies in influence show us that a minority who holds to the same position regardless of new information is not as effective as those who demonstrate some flexibility. A confident person is not afraid to reevaluate the situation. When presented with information that was not part of your original equation, take the time to consider it, without casual disregard. Then, should you find that this new information is not a mitigating factor, be bold in your declaration that your position has not changed—and, if feasible, that your position is now even stronger in light of this new information.

## Strategy 3: Emote Emotions

Ninety percent of the decisions we make are based on emotion. We then use logic to justify our actions. Think of all the useless things that you have lying around your home and office. How many of them did you really need, and how many did you just want and then convince yourself (and others) that you really do need it and can't live without it? "I'll be twice as productive!" went your sales pitch.

If you appeal to others on a strictly logical basis, you will have little chance of swaying others—no matter how sound and rational your argument is. You need to translate the facts into clear and specific benefits that appeal to the person's emotions.

In addition to arousing strong emotions, research shows that you will be especially effective when you offer a precise game plan with a clear-cut course of action for proceeding. When we are motivated to take action and move forward, it makes us feel comfortable and secure to know that the path is clearly lit and laid out. When you want to move the minority, provide more than just the desired destination; also give them a map for getting there.

---

### A Baby in a Well

A paper by Paul Slovic (2007) contrasted the overwhelming media attention and concern given to baby Jessica (the small child who was stuck in a well) and the worldwide apathy genocides abroad generated, where literally tens of thousands of people are slaughtered each week. The conclusion, which has been echoed by ensuing studies, reveals how numbers and statistics have a hard time penetrating our emotional center, while an image of a single child more easily pulls at our heartstrings. (Donations to nonprofit organizations increase when their advertising depicts a single person in need, rather than two people—much less an entire village or city.)

---

# Strategy 4: Risk Aversion

Your attempt to persuade will be considerably more successful if you emphasize how your idea will prevent negative or unpleasant consequences (Leventhal et al. 1965). Yet, one of the chief missteps we make is to focus primarily on the *benefits* that our idea would produce. We go on at length about how wonderful and great things will be once our plan is put into effect. Studies bear out that this approach may be ineffective when you are attempting to sway others to your way of thinking.

Most interesting is that negatively framed outcomes shift in favor of your plan, even when it is riskier than another course of action. Called *risky choice framing effects*, human beings are more inclined to take a risk (e.g., elect a risky medical procedure) when potential outcomes are *not* positively framed (e.g., in terms of success rate) but rather negatively framed (e.g., in terms of failure rate). Simply put, we are more disposed to take a risk to avoid a loss than to achieve a gain (Kahneman and Tversky 1979).

Your position, then, should focus primarily on how the status quo or another's suggestion will lead to unpleasant consequences;

your plan saves the company from experiencing this nasty potential outcome.

The concept of framing information to influence a person's perception of the situation extends beyond positive and negative outcomes. Let's take a look at the landmark 1981 study by Tversky and Kahmneman:

> Imagine that the U.S. is preparing for an outbreak of an unusual Asian disease, which is expected to kill 600 people. Two alternative programs to combat the disease are proposed. Assume that the exact scientific estimates of the consequences of the programs are as follows:
>
> *   If program A is adopted, 200 people will be saved.
> *   If program B is adopted, there is a 1/3 probability that 600 people will be saved and 2/3 probability that no people will be saved.

Which program would you choose? When the programs were framed in this way, the researchers found that 72 percent of the respondents chose to save 200 lives rather than risk everyone's lives. However, they then posed the question to a second group of subjects with a twist and framed the alternatives differently.

*   If program C is adopted, 400 people will die.
*   If program D is adopted, there is a 1/3 probability that nobody will die, and 2/3 probability the 600 people will die.

In surprisingly stark contrast to programs A and B, 78 percent of the respondents chose D, the riskier alternative, when presented with programs C and D. In case statistics is not your strong suit, choices A and C are exactly alike. Out of the 600 people, if *"400 people will die,"* then *"200 people will be saved."* Likewise, choices B and D offer the same odds. If there is a *"1/3 probability that 600 people will be saved,"* there is the same probability that—out of the 600—*"nobody will die."*

In the survival (or positive) frame, people are *less* likely to take risks to maintain survival. In the mortality (or negative) frame, risk taking is preferred more often to avoid death. Same information. Different presentation.

# Strategy 5: Stealing Thunder

What do you do when you know there is a weakness in your argument? Do you wait to see if someone will bring it up? Research says no. As long as it does not completely destroy your point, beating others to the proverbial punch actually gives you *more* credibility.

Stealing thunder is a tactic whereby you are the first to introduce information that is injurious to your position. It is shown to successfully dilute the impact of negative information. Interestingly, one such study, utilizing a mock trial, found that only one thing invalidated the effectiveness of this technique: when opposing counsel revealed to the mock jurors that the stealing thunder tactic had been used on them. The success of this technique hinges on our integrity as evidenced by the fact that in the interest of true justice, we are bringing up, ourselves, information that hurts our own case. However, when this tactic is exposed, it has a boomerang effect, and this very credibility is undermined because the other party feels manipulated (Dolnik et al. 2003).

# Strategy 6: So Smooth

You're making a great presentation, building consensus, and then you get thrown a curve ball. A question is asked, and you need to buy some time. The problem? You're concerned that you may come off as being unsure or unprepared if you don't respond right away with some sort of an answer. Use this four-point tactic to gracefully and eloquently deal with the challenge.

1. Smile slightly and nod approvingly to show that you are not thrown or bothered by the question.
2. Say, "That's a great question! In fact when I first thought about this very point…." This shows that you've already considered the question, but it doesn't make the person feel foolish for asking. Now the group is prepped that you've got a good answer, and they are more inclined to accept what you say.

---

### Tooting Your Own Horn

Regarding first impressions, there is something called the *primacy effect:* the process whereby our first impression of another person causes us to interpret his subsequent behavior in a manner consistent with the first impression. It's key because everything we see and hear *afterward* gets filtered through our initial opinion. Therefore, your introduction is vital. Don't do it yourself! Studies have shown that you can increase your credibility and prestige by having a third party extol your virtues and talents. However, when we attempt to present ourselves in a positive light, we are perceived as self-promoting and thus viewed unfavorably. The findings conclude that even when you are present and even when the third party has a clear and obvious conflict of interest, you are still viewed more favorably than those who self-promote (Pfeffer et al. 2006).

---

3. Make the question *more difficult* to answer. "Let's not ask what happens if the return rate exceeds my projection by 5 percent, but let's make your question stronger. What happens if it is as high as 10 percent?" This tactic also engages the listeners' heuristic programming. In brief, as a way of digesting the vast amounts of information that we are exposed to and making competent decisions, our brain takes short-cuts. For example, would you like a free diamond ring? Or maybe you would rather have an aluminum can? Which do you want *more*, and *why?* Of course, the ring, which you perceive as more valuable because of its utility and degree of availability. Generally speaking, that which is rare is more valuable and expensive, even though this may not always be so. Aunt Harriet's handwritten autobiography is certainly rare—one of a kind—but not worth too much in cash. As applied here, whenever a person makes his own job—in this case the question—harder, our brains suspend processing and falsely assume that he must really know his stuff.

4. Now you give the best answer you've got. By following the previous three steps, you've bought yourself some time, and via the law of expectancy you *increased* the impression that you are in control of the facts. It almost doesn't matter what you say as even a general nonanswer will be heard as authoritative and positive.

See also:

- Chapter 18: *Master the Art of Charisma with the Complete Psychological Formula for Instant Likability*

# 18

## Master the Art of Charisma with the Complete Psychological Formula for Instant Likability

*"Charisma is seductive. And everyone is seducible."*

—August F. Livingston

Wikipedia comes as close to a definition of *charisma* as we're likely to get:

> Although difficult or even impossible to define accurately (due to an abundance of wildly diverse criteria in regard to the trait), charisma is often used to describe an elusive, even undefinable personality trait that often includes the seemingly "supernatural" or uncanny ability to lead, charm, persuade, inspire, and/or influence people. It refers especially to a quality in certain people who easily draw the attention and admiration of others due to a "magnetic" quality of personality and/or appearance.

Undeniably, charisma, or having the ability to be instantly liked by almost anyone, is an invaluable tool because likability is a dominant force in the workplace, from promotions, to sales, to negotiations. Here we'll explore how minor changes in your behavior—from imperceptible to apparent—can radically alter how others perceive you.

## Strategy 1: You're Just Like Me

Only in the past few decades have we begun to decipher the subtle components of human rapport. Although many good books discuss the subject, here we examine the deeper psychology behind its real strength and influence. Let's take a look.

Rapport is silent power that allows us to alter how we are perceived—a synchronized reflection of another that can build emotional affinity and even exert extreme influence.

When you mirror a person—their behavior, values, traits, appearance, speech, in fact, anything—he sees a reflection of himself in you. His brain registers: *You are me*, and people who are like each other tend to like each other.

Mimicry's subtle powers of persuasion have deep neurophysiological roots. According to University of Chicago neuroscientist

Jean Decety, mimicry activates brain circuits that are known to be involved in feelings of empathy. Decety's studies use functional magnetic resonance imaging (fMRI) technology to peer inside the brains of subjects and investigate the neural substrates of emotion.

Decety says that a similar empathetic neural response occurs when a person takes pleasure in the good fortune of a friend or enjoys a conversation partner. "When you're being mimicked in a good way," he says, "it communicates a kind of pleasure, a social high you're getting from the other person."

---

### Drinking It In

In a 2008 study, Robin Tanner and Tanya Chartrand, psychologists at Duke, demonstrated how social mimicry can influence the behavior of a potential client or investor. Thirty-seven Duke students were asked to taste a new sports drink named Vigor and answer questions about the product. The interviewer mirrored the posture and movement of about half the participants. Participants who were mimicked by the interviewer rated Vigor more favorably—and drank more of it—than participants who were not mimicked. The mimicked participants were also more likely to say they would buy Vigor and to predict that it would be successful in the marketplace.

---

Even more intriguing, a separate experiment showed that both product ratings and consumption rate increased even more when the interviewer-mimicker expressly stated that he was invested in the success of the product. This is, as Chartrand points out, somewhat counterintuitive. "Normally, you'd expect that if people realize someone is invested in a product and trying to sell it to them, they'd be less enthusiastic. But we found that people who were mimicked actually felt more strongly about the product when they knew the other person was invested in it" (Meltzoff and Decety 2003).

Extensive research conducted by Jeremy Bailenson, a cognitive psychologist at Stanford, demonstrates that successful mimickers need not even be human. Bailenson's goal was to determine how astute people are in detecting digital chameleons—that is, computer agents or avatars who mimic them—and examine the social implications of mimicry detection (Bailenson et al. 2008).

Research participants interacted with a realistic-looking avatar inside an immersive virtual reality simulation. The avatar delivered a three-minute persuasive verbal presentation to participants, coming across as warm and convincing, as if controlled by another human. For half the participants, the agent was a digital chameleon—its head movements were an exact mimicry of the participant's head movements, presented at a four-second delay. The other half of the participants viewed a prerecorded presentation: The avatar's head movements were a mimicry of another participant's head movements.

Following the avatar's presentation, the participants were asked questions and presented with an agent impression scale. The results demonstrated two important findings: (1) Only 5 percent of all participants realized they were being mimicked, and (2) participants were more persuaded by the avatar, liked the avatar more, and actually watched the avatar more intensely when the avatar was mimicking them, as opposed to mimicking someone else.

"Turns out, humans are extremely poor at detecting when people or technology are mimicking them," Bailenson says. "A person or computer agent has the ability to move like us or smile like us and we have no idea it's occurring, yet it's a uniquely powerful strategy for anyone who's trying to teach us, sell us or persuade us." We feel unconsciously drawn to this person.

Since we tend to take what we see at face value, can our behavior be shaped by deliberately false information? Bailenson explored this question in a 2004 experiment conducted in collaboration with Stanford's Political Communication Lab. Bailenson's researchers morphed photos of undecided voters with those of either George Bush or John Kerry, using a 30 to 40 percent morph ratio. Voters preferred the candidate whom they had been morphed into, *but not a single one of the 2,500 participants realized that their own likenesses had been melded into the photo they chose.*

In Bailenson's avatar experiments, subjects detected the mimicry only when it was immediate and precise. If the avatar's behavior was slightly out of sync—say, by four seconds—the mimicking went undetected. Bailenson's research showed that waiting four seconds before imitating someone's head movements makes that person much more likely to like you and to agree with you.

Getting it right is a delicate balance, Bailenson says. "Really good salespeople, and for that matter good con artists, have known about these skills and used them forever. I suspect that people who are good at this know how to do it intuitively."

So, what's the magic time delay formula for rapport-building mimicry? Start by mirroring head nods, a socially acceptable— perhaps even expected—behavior that has a low risk of being perceived as mimicry, even if detected, and begin with longer time delays of four to six seconds. Monitor the dynamic in the room keenly, and gradually refine your timing.

## Strategy 2: How You Make Her Feel

You can spend all day trying to get her to like you and to think well of you, but it's how you make her feel when she is around you that makes the difference. Have you ever noticed how nice it is to be around someone who is complimentary and sincerely kind and warm? Conversely, think about how annoying it is to spend five minutes with a person who's always finding fault with everything and everyone. These people seem to drain the life right out of you. Being the person who makes people feel good will go a long way toward infusing yourself with the mysterious aura of charisma. We elaborate on one such way to do this—the power of a simple smile—at the end of this chapter.

At the expense of stating the obvious, here are some other ways as outlined by way of one of the greatest relationship experts, Dale Carnegie, in *How to Win Friends and Influence People* (1936).

- Become genuinely interested in other people.
- Smile.

- Remember that a person's name is to that person the sweetest and most important sound in any language.
- Be a good listener. Encourage others to talk about themselves.
- Talk in terms of the other person's interests.
- Make the other person feel important—and do it sincerely.

Few of us would be taken aback by any of these intuitive, even commonsense suggestions. We know them, but we don't always use them, and we need to remind ourselves that making other people feel good about themselves is the most direct path to their feeling good about us.

## Strategy 3: He's Only Human

Setting yourself up as someone who is better than the rest is giving those around you the incentive to hope that you fail. The most intoxicating ingredient in the charisma mix is humility. As we saw earlier, when our ego is not engaged, we easily and directly connect to others. An arrogant person, by contrast, is too full of himself to make room for anyone else.

Do not make the mistake of thinking that humility is weakness. It is strength. An arrogant person only takes. He is an emotional junkie, depending on others to feed his fragile ego, and a slave to his own impulses that he cannot rise above.

How does one acquire humility? To be humble by putting ourselves in humbling situations is like a person choosing to sleep the night in a homeless shelter: While positive, it is voluntary. He is in control and, as such, is not really humbled. In fact, he may now think to himself, *Look what I was able to do.*

When a person has been thrust into a situation where he is not in control and maintains self-control by exercising free will, however, he gains lasting humility. To manufacture conditions where we are dependent does not really demonstrate anything about our character—since it was our free will to enter that situation.

A wealthy person begging for money on the street has only a mild opportunity to enhance his humility. On the other hand, when the same person is in a naturally humbling situation—for example, he finds himself on the street without his wallet—and instead of becoming frustrated and upset by his inability to give charity, he rises above his nature, he radiates true humility.

When you find yourself in a difficult or embarrassing situation and respond with poise and grace, you radiate charisma but infuse yourself with greater humility. You will not be seen as weak but as someone who is truly strong, and this strength will inspire others to attach themselves to you.

## Six Keys to Humility

1. When you or those around you think a job is beneath you, do it anyway. This shows the people around you that you are a person of the people who is willing to make sacrifices for the greater good. When you go out of your way to check on an order and ensure it's delivered on the scheduled date, a task that another employee could have done, you exemplify humility. The company president who tosses his own trash in the proper recycle bin or who picks up garbage off the cafeteria floor inspires the company's workers to do the same.

2. Nothing brings out awe like someone admitting he was wrong. If you have made a mistake, publicly acknowledge it and give credit to the person who was right. If an error occurs with a client or customer, regardless of how small, be the first to call and apologize. Let her know the steps you have taken to rectify the situation and assure her that with these steps now in place, it won't happen again.

3. This one also falls into the *don't pretend you know everything* category. If you don't know the answer to a question, don't make up an answer. "I don't know" will suffice, and you'll be amazed at the number of people who will pay attention. When a customer or client asks you a question and you don't know the answer, reply, "I don't know, but I'll find out for you." Then follow through, and keep him up to date with the progress.

4. Treat everyone with respect, and that means even people you don't need anything from or who can't do anything for you. Ignoring someone who is seemingly unimportant only shows our smallness. People like and respect those who make them feel good, important, and needed.

5. When you make a mistake, smile at yourself. Don't try to ignore it or pretend it didn't happen. Self-deprecating humor is a terrific way to ingratiate yourself with anyone. When you show others that you don't take yourself so seriously, it makes them feel closer to you and want to be around you. Nobody likes a show-off or a person who is so consumed with himself and his image that he needs to pretend that he is perfect. We like and gravitate toward those who are not self-absorbed and egotistical. Showing that you can laugh at yourself makes you entirely more approachable and charismatic.

6. Another dimension of human design is that it is not just the visibly defenseless and helpless with whom we can readily connect. When a person exhibits a tremendous degree of self-sacrifice and puts his own needs or even his life to the side for another, we get that lump-in-the-throat feeling. Why? Because that person has set aside his own ego; he has given of himself to do what is right for another person, and so we are touched.

This connection does not come from a sense of the other's vulnerability but, rather, his infinite goodness. A charismatic personality is fortified by putting others ahead of his own needs. When you engage in such self-sacrifice, you become irresistibly attractive, and others are automatically drawn to you.

## Strategy 4: The Strength of Morality

We are rapt and captivated by those who have a strong sense of right and wrong.

Your moral backbone shows throughout the day in a variety of ways. When you are unwavering in your commitment to the truth, people will be unwavering in their affinity for you. For instance, share the credit and make others look good. Whenever you are acknowledged for your work, be sure to mention every other person who contributed to your success, even in a small way. When a client congratulates you on a job well done, and you respond with, *"Thank you, but credit must really be shared with Jim and Susan,"* you will be a superhero.

---

### Keep Away from Workplace Gossip

If people are gossiping, walk away. Taking in gossip just makes you look, well, cheap. We respect people who do not talk about others. It shows a strong moral core, and, as noted earlier, we are attracted to, trust, and appreciate people who are principled.

---

When your own boss tells you that you did a great job on a project, and you bring your subordinate into the office and say, "I appreciate your kind words, Mr. Green, but I want you to know that Tim Brown here deserves much of the credit," they will both see you in a positive light. Being capable is good, and many people are capable. Acting from a true moral center is great, and few people do so. It will set you apart and brand you as a person with that indefinable something.

## Strategy 5: A Positive Attitude

As we discussed earlier, we like people who are similar to us. But there is one exception to this rule. Nobody wants to be around a moody, angry-at-the-world pessimist. We all seek, like, and admire those who have a positive, happy outlook and perspective on life. Why? Because that is what we all want. And seeing this desirable spirit in others makes us like them more. You may know a person—or may even be someone—who is annoyed by those who wake up smiling and in a good mood. The fact is, though, at some level we are drawn to that attitude and to that person.

Think of the people in your life you really can't stand to be around. Chances are they are always complaining about something, always annoyed with somebody, always finding fault with everything. Like confidence, a positive attitude will help to turn you into a super-human magnet for attracting people.

Doesn't misery love company? Actually, it does. Miserable people like to be around people who are just as annoyed with life as they are. But this quality does not make them like these people more. Someone who feels miserable enjoys commiserating and complaining with another miserable individual, but the minute he's in a good mood, he will abandon the toxic, annoying person. He seeks solace with somebody who feels as he does, but when he no longer feels that way, he will instantly leave this relationship. This is because he never liked the person (at least not for this similarity); he enjoyed only the shared attitude.

## Strategy 6: The Power of a Smile!

The number one tactic for emanating charisma is the easiest to do: *Smile!* Smiling accomplishes four powerful things: It conveys *confidence, happiness,* and *enthusiasm* and, most important, it shows *acceptance*.

Psychologist Daniel Goleman (2002) writes, "It happens that smiles are the most contagious emotional signal of all, having an almost irresistible power to make other people smile in return." If you, upon seeing someone you know, walk over with a big smile and a genuine sign of pleasure for being with her, you will make her feel like a million dollars. She will, in turn, show vast appreciation for your making her feel so comfortable, welcomed, and regarded.

The importance of initially setting the right tone cannot be overstated. In every type of relationship, those few moments when you first come into a meeting or come across a colleague or client shape the quality of this encounter in a most dramatic way.

People who smile are also perceived as *confident* because when we are nervous or unsure about ourselves or our surroundings, we tend not to smile. Smiling, of course, conveys *happiness,* and we are drawn to happy people: We simply view them more favorably. Enthusiasm boosts a charismatic personality because it's *contagious*. Your smile shows that you are pleased to be where you are, and others in turn become more excited with being around you.

## A Trusting Smile

How does a smile's *speed* affect its perception? In an experiment, 100 participants sat in front of a monitor to judge the smiles of synthetic faces. They watched the faces smiling—some whose smile appeared in just over 0.1 of a second and others whose smile appeared in just over 0.5 of a second. Participants then expressed their opinions as to how trustworthy, attractive, fake, and flirtatious the smiles made the faces seem. The researchers found long-onset smiles were perceived as more attractive and trustworthy (Krumhuber et al. 2007).

Smiling conveys a type of *acceptance* that lets the other person know that from where we're standing, he's okay. Because most of us are walking around feeling deficient or defective in one way or another, a sincere smile helps us feel good about who we are and, in turn, generates a strong affinity toward you.

See also:

- Chapter 7: *Turn a Saboteur into Your Greatest Ally*
- Chapter 17: *Sway the Room: From Jury Rooms to Board Rooms, How One Voice Can Change the Choir*
- Chapter 19: *The Amazing Method for Getting Along with People Who Are Emotionally Unwell*

# 19

## The Amazing Method for Getting Along with People Who Are Emotionally Unwell

*"I became insane, with long periods of horrible sanity."*

—Edgar Allen Poe (1809–1849)

The workplace in corporate America can more effectively weed out these types of people, but in small businesses, particularly family-run businesses, highly neurotic and unstable people can torpedo a successful business all too quickly. So what do we do?

If you are dealing with someone who is truly emotionally unwell, consider the following to make your life and your job infinitely easier: *It is not your job to teach him reality.* Unless he is actively working on his clarity and well-being, he will not ever wake up, apologize, and say, "I've been a fool, you're right. I don't know what I've been thinking all of these years." This is a fantasy. It will not happen.

Regardless of the person's accomplishments, he is still mentally ill. You have to really understand this. There is nothing you can say or do that will increase his emotional capacity. Just as a physically handicapped person cannot do certain things, one who is emotionally handicapped cannot do certain things. You will never make him see things differently than he does now. Do not expect that he will change his attitude, opinion, or outlook.

Your objective is to have as cordial and productive a relationship as possible, not to educate.

Once you accept his capacity—which may be extremely limited—you will more easily relate to him. Make a decision now. Do you want to have the best relationship possible with this person, or do you want to be right and try to prove it to him, time and again? Many encounters will come down to a decision between showing you are right and being effective. You cannot do both.

## Is It Really a Relationship?

Just because two people are related or have interacted with each other, does that mean there's a relationship? A relationship is two people, each giving and receiving. If a person is unable to give to you and is only taking, then you don't have a relationship—you have a one person giving and one person taking. We become so angry because we believe it to be a relationship. If the other person is not capable of giving, then your expectations will always exceed the confines of his ability, and you will be perpetually frustrated and disappointed. If, instead, you reframe the dynamic and consider your help, advice, support, and understanding to be an act of kindness to a sick person rather than a relationship, then you will not be distressed when your needs are not met. The definition makes a big difference.

Many of us have had the experience of speaking to someone who is, by all appearances, quite bright, but she simply is not getting it. We think that if we just present a rational argument and explain the facts clearly and logically, then this person cannot draw anything other than the right conclusion and then see things our way—the right way.

This thinking is more illogical than that of the person we wish to persuade. This other person is not thinking, so reasons and rationale have no place. He is feeling, and while emotionally charged, he does not see reality and cannot hear you. So, ironically, who is really more out of touch with reality? This person who cannot hear the truth, or we who try to sway him, in spite of the fact that he will not listen to reason? The other person cannot help himself in this situation. We know better and can avoid futility.

We all have our blind spots, areas of life where we do not let reality in. Yet it seems ridiculous or even crazy to us when others act irrationally, only because their blind spots are different than ours. We are just as crazy—more so, in fact, if we choose to not accept what is and instead become angry, frustrated, and annoyed when someone else is simply not hearing us.

For happier and more harmonious relationships, keep in mind that we all have moments when we simply do not see reality clearly, and the greatest argument in the world may not be enough to make us face what we need to see.

Adjusting your attitude and perspective is paramount. Although you will not cure anyone by changing how you relate to them, you will greatly enhance your ability to enjoy the best-quality relationship possible.

# Strategy 1: The Six-Facet Approach

A great deal of your approach depends on the nature of the interaction, as well as how far off emotionally the other person is. Despite the multitude of variables, there are some solid psychological tools for building the best relationship possible.

1. Show enthusiasm for being around her. If she gets the impression that it is a chore for you to have a conversation with her, it will eat away at her emotional well-being and at the bond between you.

2. Show appreciation for her ideas and her time. When you speak with her, give your full attention to the conversation. And be diligent in thanking her for her opinions and ideas, regardless of whether you agree with them.

3. Be attentive to her needs and comfort. Even something simple, such as getting her a glass of water if she seems thirsty, goes miles toward making her feel good about herself and her relationship with you.

4. Someone who is emotionally unbalanced often does not trust herself and her own judgment. When you show that you trust her, she regains a sense of worth and confidence in herself. Ask for her advice and input. Get her opinion on things. It gives her a chance to give, and this helps her feel self-reliant. It is best, too, to seek out this person's advice and help with something that will not cause the end of the world if things don't go the way you had hoped.

5. Have her help you with a project or assignment. Solicit her help to give her a chance to contribute to something and someone else. Instability creates a mode of self-absorption and sometimes

narcissistic behavior. Taking the focus off her and her own problems gives her a healthier perspective.

6. Help her feel a sense of control and freedom in what she does and how she lives her life. A mind without an active, productive focus can inflate a minor concern or stress until it consumes all our time and attention. If the situation allows, let her be in charge as much as possible. Sometimes we want to help this person to alleviate unnecessary stress, but in doing so we create a larger sense of dependency. Give her the ability to be in charge of herself or of a specific area as much as you can. Ask her to do something and give her full autonomy in its planning and execution—from beginning to end.

---

### The Friendly Skies

Flight attendants begin each trip by informing passengers that in an emergency situation, those traveling with children should secure their own oxygen masks first and only then secure the masks on their children. We are no good to anyone else if we are no good to ourselves. Whenever we redraw lines in relationships, one person gets less territory; however, without boundaries, there is no definition of self. While some relationships benefit from having no boundaries, allowing those who are toxic to make the rules is not healthy. In certain rare instances, then, we are obligated to say, "Enough is enough."

---

## Wait! Why Be Bothered in the First Place?

Linguists recognize a sentence that is illogical if it is semantically incorrect. Consider the statement "My friend forced me to have blue eyes." No one would accept this sentence as truthful. However, we easily accept the declaration "My friend makes me angry." Both statements, though, are semantically identical and, according to linguists, structurally incorrect.

A short-term therapy called neuro linguistic programming (NLP) recognizes the need to identify such destructive patterns because of their inherent tendency to pervade our subconscious thoughts. The creators of NLP offer in *The Structure of Magic* (Bandler and Grinder 1975) the following overview as an aid, designed for therapists, to recognize when this behavior is present:

> We have generalized the notion of semantic ill-formedness to include sentences such as:
>
> *My husband makes me mad.*
>
> The therapist can identify this sentence as having the form:
>
> *Some person causes some person to have some emotion.*
>
> When the first person, the one doing the causing, is different from the person experiencing the anger, the sentence is said to be semantically ill-formed and unacceptable. The semantic ill-formedness of sentences of this type arises because, it, literally, **is not possible for one human being to create an emotion in another human being**—thus, we reject sentences of this form. Sentences of this type, in fact, identify situations in which one person does some act and a second person *responds* by feeling a certain way. The point here is that, although the two events occur one after another, there is no necessary connection between the act of one person and the response of the other.
>
> Therefore, sentences of this type identify a model in which the client assigns responsibility for his emotion; rather, the emotion is a response generated from the model in which the client takes no responsibility for experiences which he *could* control.

We assume that an event is to blame for our feelings; this is not so. The bottom line: You don't have to be annoyed because someone does something annoying. You choose your own response.

See also:

- Chapter 9: *Managing Difficult People: The Psychology Behind Royal Pains*
- Chapter 20: *Instantly Resolve Any Personality Conflict*

# 20

## Instantly Resolve Any Personality Conflict

*"In business, when two people always agree, one of them is irrelevant."*

—William Wrigley Jr. (1861–1932)

Personality conflicts at work can run the gamut from very petty concerns to disastrous results that can affect not only the individuals but other employees as well. These clashes can cause distractions that make it impossible for work to get done on time and uncomfortable for the workers, for management, and for clients who come into the workplace.

Mood and morale can be lowered as a result of these types of conflicts, and teamwork can come apart at the seams. All supervisors have to keep in mind that conflicts often have a ripple effect in an office and must be dealt with immediately before they start affecting productivity.

---

### Did You Know?

What about those times when the conflict isn't so great but the two people involved just seem to either resent each other or are easily annoyed by the other person? This situation is completely about respect; there are no real issues to deal with. You can make peace very easily and effectively by telling each person how much the other really respects the way he does or did something. You will find, almost every single time, that each person—who now feels respected by the other—begins to act with significant kindness and respect for the other.

---

Some conflicts are easier to resolve than others. For garden-variety issues, a supervisor can bring both individuals into her office and speak to them to find out the source of the conflict and how to resolve it in a fair and timely fashion. This often works, as does issuing a cease-and-desist warning to both parties. This tactic may prove to be more effective than a surface read reveals because neither party has to be concerned with saving face by defending his behavior or escalating the conflict. Each can feel that he is ceasing because he has to, not because he is backing down.

Alas, some conflicts are not so easily resolved.

If a conflict keeps escalating, then first try a tactical approach, such as finding a way to separate the individuals. You can move their desks far apart or have them work different shifts. More drastically, one person can be transferred to another section of the building or another office. You can offer professional anger management courses or conflict resolution workshops to both parties if you think that might help.

It doesn't much matter if any one person is at fault, because the one who is responsible clearly doesn't see it this way. We can assume there was a difference of opinion over who did what to whom and who is to blame for what. Or it may be just a general lack of respect for one another that is manifested in conversations filled with sarcastic remarks and an underlying air of hostility, competition, or jealousy.

Your overall objective is to give information about each party to the other—information that will change how each person sees the other and consequently interacts with and treats the other.

## The Three-Phase Approach Strategy

You can use any of the phases separately, combine any two of the phases, or use all three.

### Phase 1: Reestablish Respect

Let each person know that the other really respects the way he does a particular thing or admires something he stands for or supports. In almost every situation, the reason one person treats the other with a lack of respect is simply that he doesn't feel he gets respect from the other person.

### Phase 2: Demonstrate Consequences

Let each one know that although the other didn't say anything to you outright, you know that each cares a great deal about what the other thinks of him, and he might want to lighten up a bit. Maybe give some nice words of encouragement, which you know will go a long way and make him feel good.

## Phase 3: Humanize

It's good to let the other know things—as long as it doesn't violate one's trust and confidence in the other. When we learn that someone was a war veteran, had a tragedy when young, or is suffering an illness, we can't help being more compassionate and empathetic, regardless of what we think of him.

---

### External Threat

Numerous studies conclude that division among people dissolves in the face of an outside threat. Civil war, intrasocietal conflicts, and internal unrest often cease when a common external enemy comes onto the scene. Conversely, individuals more often turn their attention and hostility to one another when no such forces are present. The fastest way to instill cooperation between two people is to (1) create an external focus and/or (2) set your group against another group in some form of competition.

---

For example, a school principal has two teachers who don't get along well. He's not sure what caused the problem, and he doesn't believe he'd get a straight answer if he asked. He simply wants to get them to become friendlier and work together better. (Teacher 1 is the cause of most of the friction.)

### Principal to Teacher 1

**Principal:** I've got to tell you, I know that you and Teacher 2 don't always see eye-to-eye on things, but I think some of the remarks you make really upset her.

**Teacher 1:** Really? I didn't say anything that rude. Maybe she's just sensitive.

**Principal:** I know, but I happen to know that she has a great deal of respect for you, and the comments sting a bit when they come from someone she really wants to impress.

**Teacher 1:** Oh, okay. I never realized.

**Principal:** I know. So any words of encouragement are going to mean an awful lot to her. Besides, she's been through a lot with her son, who's been in and out of the hospital for the past few years.

## Principal to Teacher 2

**Principal:** You know, I was speaking with Teacher 1 about the upcoming parent conference, and she suggested that I ask you for your thoughts. [He explains what's going on and then adds] I know that you and Teacher 1 have had your moments, but she thinks you're an excellent teacher.

See also:

- Chapter 9: *Managing Difficult People: The Psychology Behind Royal Pains*
- Chapter 18: *Master the Art of Charisma with the Complete Psychological Formula for Instant Likability*
- Chapter 19: *The Amazing Method for Getting Along with People Who Are Emotionally Unwell*

# 21

## The Effortless Way to Make Difficult Changes without Creating Fearful, Frustrated, and Angry Employees

*"Change is inevitable—except from a vending machine."*
—Robert C. Gallagher

The overall psychological strategy to making unpleasant changes includes acquiring the ability to inspire an employee to do an undesirable task, willingly and perhaps even happily. The following approaches will help you to maximize your leverage to accomplish this.

## Strategy 1: Encourage Volunteering

When we choose to do something, we are unconsciously driven to like it more. Otherwise, why would we be doing it? We prefer not to think that we made a mistake in choosing, do something.

Abundant investigations in the phenomenon of hazing provide proof for what most of us knew all along. These findings confirmed that the more unpleasant the process members underwent to get into a group, the better they liked the group, and the stronger their commitment and allegiance to it.

For example, let's say a person gave away everything she owned, including her money, and disposed of all her friends so she could become a member of a new cult with the promise that she would find the meaning of life. Once reality sets in, she has a choice to make: She is going to believe she has just done the dumbest thing ever, or she is going to believe that the cult is where she belongs.

Even if she knows deep down that tossing away her life, friends, money, and possessions was wrong, she, like most people, more often takes the course of minimal emotional resistance. She comes to the conclusion that she made the right choice and that she will now bide her time and wait for the mother ship to arrive. By contrast, if someone had held a gun to her head and *forced* her to join, then she does not have to take on the responsibility of trying to justify her behavior.

To capitalize on this function of human behavior, investigate ways to get employees to sign up for the new position or opportunity. The act of volunteering will positively and permanently skew their attitude to favor the new conditions.

# Strategy 2: Developing an Intrinsic Desire

In a previous chapter, we spoke of the importance of intrinsic motivators over extrinsic ones. This concept becomes even more necessary when you go beyond keeping an employee content under current conditions and move to keeping an employee happy and motivated in a new, possibly unpleasant, atmosphere. There are three components in the process of maximizing intrinsic motivation.

## 1. Put the Task into a Larger Context

A man walking by a construction site comes upon a bricklayer and inquires, "What are you doing?" The worker responds, "I'm laying bricks." As he walks along, he asks the same question to another worker, who answers, "I'm laying the foundation for a big beautiful building." Finally, as he leaves the site, he asks the same question of a third bricklayer, who beams proudly and says, "Me? I'm helping to build a state-of-the-art children's hospital where kids from around

### Feelings, Nothing More Than Feelings

Breakthrough research on memory and feelings is currently being conducted by James McGaugh, a professor of neurobiology at the University of California, Irvine. When a person experiences a disturbing event, they feel intense fear and helplessness, which stimulates adrenaline. The result is that even years later, strong feelings remain. The drug propranolol sits on the nerve cell and blocks the production of adrenaline; it is adrenaline that intensifies an experience and keeps it locked in a heightened state in memory. Therefore, even after the fact, people who received this adrenaline-blocking drug while thinking about a past trauma were able to form a new association to the event and, in some instances, transform their feelings toward it. It becomes clear, then, that it is not the circumstances, but rather *our thoughts about the situation*, that give rise to the emotions that determine an event's impact and lasting influence.

the world will be able to come to get the latest and most advanced treatment for their sickness."

Who do you think is more motivated to go to work each day? Whenever we do something that has meaning, it gives meaning to our lives, and meaning is pleasurable. Everything in creation serves a purpose beyond itself. Every cell in the human body and every drop of water in the ocean is in a symbiotic relationship with the larger organism; it is an integral part of a larger purpose, serving an even greater function.

You activate someone else's intrinsic motivation when you help him become a part of something that connects him to a larger whole. If a person feels isolated in his job, like a cog in a wheel that he cannot see, understand, or relate to, then he cannot feel passionate about his job.

## 2. A Sense of Control

According to research (Holmes and Rahe 1967), individuals with high life change scores (indicating that a person is experiencing multiple changes in his life at one time) are more likely to fall ill, but the most surprising aspect is that illness correlates with *any type of change*. Whether the event is positive or negative has no effect on the stress experienced; the circumstances are largely irrelevant, but the ability to feel in control is imperative.

This is exactly why we may find ourselves engaging in self-destructive behavior, even when life is going well; it is not about the circumstances, it's about whether we feel the need to control the situation.

The implications are far-reaching. Whether a person experiences something positive, such a promotion, or something negative, such as a layoff, the stress associated with the event has little or nothing to do with the circumstances, but rather with our ability to feel some control over the experience.

Garner your employee input, and offer, to whatever degree you can, alternatives. Even where the options are equally unpleasant, the fact that the person has *some* say in his fate gives him a sense of empowerment, which goes a long way toward alleviating the stress associated with these changes. In addition, this bit of power stimulates the intrinsic aspect involved in volunteering, as discussed in the first strategy.

### 3. A Feeling of Progress

The ego needs measurable traction; it wants results it can feel proud of and evidence that it is effective. A drop in the ocean does not inspire us, but results with a tangible, visible payoff lead to the desire to invest more of ourselves and work harder. It is not enough for this person to get the feeling that things are happening; when the going gets tough, his ego needs to point to indisputable, concrete proof that he is making a real, consequential, and permanent impact.

Having been thrust into new circumstances, your employee needs to feel the full weight of the relationship between cause and effect. Devise a quantifiable way to measure progress, so that his focus is directed toward producing a positive outcome rather than on the situation itself.

In our own lives as well, when we have a goal, something to move toward, we are less bothered and frustrated by circumstances. However, when we feel stagnant or that our efforts make little difference, then everything little thing bothers us.

Imagine you are playing a competitive, exciting sport. At a certain point in the game, you become injured, but because you are so focused on the sport, you do not feel the pain. Of course, after the game, or the following day, you feel your injury, but as long as you are in the game, you are not distracted by pain. Now let us imagine a different scenario. While you are still actively involved in the sport, no one is keeping score. It has to feel a little futile. Yes, you are getting exercise and perhaps enjoying yourself, but without a way to measure success—even if you're not the competitive type—the game doesn't offer the same level of pleasure. If you get a splinter, or if the weather changes suddenly, you will more immediately notice the pain or the temperature change. You are simply not as engaged in what you are doing.

Everything in nature has a cycle. If you can actually finish something you started, not only do you gain a sense of accomplishment but also you feel more fulfilled from having seen something through to the end. So ideally, progress should come in the form of completing segments of your objective so your mini-successes are self-contained and continue to lift your intrinsic motivation and job satisfaction.

# Strategy 3: Physics of the Mind—Change by Default

Newton's first law of motion speaks to the tendency of a body in motion to stay in motion because of the property of inertia. To take advantage of this law, make what you want employees to do initially easy and straightforward; even better, you can virtually ensure getting a person to move in the right direction by making that course the path of least resistance.

According to Thaler and Sunstein (2008), research found that in one company, just 20 percent of employees had enrolled in a retirement plan after three months of employment. The form was then redesigned to make enrollment the *default* option, and participation shot above 90 percent. We're not talking about a choice between Italian food and Chinese food for lunch. Our quality of life in the golden years can be so easily manipulated, all without an ounce of perceived pressure.

Another interesting finding offered in their book *Nudge* (2008) was that placing fruit at eye level in school cafeterias enhances its popularity—and therefore its selectability—by as much as 25 percent. The authors write:

> The first thing managers have to do is harness the power of inertia. In a work setting, this could mean framing assignments so that the option perceived to be the path of least resistance is, sneakily, the one designed to get the bulk of the work done. For example, employees could be asked to either use a template to canvass a large group of people for their opinions on a given product, or compile the research and run a workshop, showing higher-ups why they should change their thinking about that product's launch. Most will likely opt for the structured—or templated—assignment, but the work gets properly done with a minimum of fuss.

# Strategy 4: Altering the Initial Impact

Four factors influence how well news is digested. When someone becomes upset about a change of circumstance, her reaction is most often due to one or more of three cognitive beliefs: (1) She perceives the situation as permanent, (2) she believes that it is crucial and much more significant than it truly is, and (3) she believes it to be *all-consuming*, that it will take over all of the other areas in her life until it is all that is left.

When any or all of these beliefs are involved, our anxiety or anger levels are more likely to increase. On the other hand, when we see a situation as *temporary or minute*, it bothers us less. Of course, the kind of news will determine how this can best be utilized, but if you can appeal to at least one of these, you will be able to reduce the negative reaction.

A fourth factor has to do with the actual words used to convey the initial message. Language, as we saw earlier, has a huge effect on how we view things and, as a result, how we feel about the things we hear. Because of this impact, a good salesperson will never say to you, *"Sign the contract."* Instead, he might suggest that you read over and okay the paperwork. Never mind that the words mean the same thing; it feels different. In own lives, we often do the same thing, sometimes subconsciously.

The language we use changes the way we perceive reality. Because *we see the world through these words*, it's always a good idea to choose our words carefully. Harsh language is something to avoid, especially words with a strong negative connotation. By avoiding those kinds of words, you will ultimately avoid an automatic reaction—like we often have to signing contracts—and help the person internalize the information more objectively, if not optimistically.

The mind can be shocked just as the body goes into shock if it is overcome with pain. On the other hand, if the information is given with softer words, the news delivers less of a shock.

## Strategy 5: Social Proof

When information is vague or has obscure implications, we don't know exactly how we should react. For instance, if you're in a crowded store and someone screams, "Fire," how do you think you'd respond? Research has shown that if everyone else remained in the store, then you would most likely remain as well. However, if everyone else suddenly bolted for the door in a frenzy, you would probably join the panicked exit.

When we are unsure of the meaning of something, we look to the world and those around us to interpret its significance. Your relaxed and casual attitude signals that this is not something that anyone should become alarmed about.

Infomercials are a multibillion-dollar industry where each second is carefully scripted for utmost impact. Legendary program writer Colleen Szot shattered a 20-year sales record for a home-shopping channel with the change of just a few words. Instead of the familiar call to action of "Operators are standing by, please call now," she rewrote the script to "If operators are busy, please call again." The message implied, of course, that others are calling in droves, so much so that you might not even be able to get through right away. That's social proof.

## Strategy 6: This Could Be Great!

Regardless of how bleak the new reality appears—whether your employee is being demoted or sent to a far-flung region—offer a real, true, specific plan on how he can do more than just make the best of a bad situation. Demonstrate how the new circumstances contain the possibility, if not the probability, for opportunities far greater than what he could have otherwise enjoyed.

When you discuss the changes, include a clear and detailed plan for the employee(s) to *experience a net gain*. Offer a concrete appreciation that while this job, on the surface, may not appear ideal, it affords the opportunity to gain experience that colleagues will not have. This, in the end, could give her the ability to ultimately rise faster and higher within the company.

## Strategy 7: The New Norm

It takes time for people to process change; but the remarkable thing is, that once we do, our attitude and expectations quickly adjust themselves—higher or lower—to accommodate our new reality.

Therefore, *keep a strong positive in the hole*—you do not want to fire all of your good news bullets at once. The reason: No matter what you say, the scales are not going to tip wildly in the favor of *"Wow, this is great."* However, because of how human beings process change, once the person adjusts to the new circumstances, *then* you can, to a great extent, affect his attitude by bringing a spot of good news into the equation. The following study illustrates just how powerful this law is.

Big lottery winners often lead miserable lives after their windfall. The statistically uneven number of suicides, murders, drunk-driving arrests, divorces, and even bankruptcies that befall lottery winners has led to studies of a lottery curse. Research showed that although people have strong emotional reactions to major changes in their lives, these reactions appear to subside more or less completely, and often quite quickly. After a period of adjustment, lottery winners are not much happier (and some are even quite miserable) than a control group.

So potent is the ability of human beings to adjust, this same study found that recent paraplegics were not much unhappier than

---

### Don't Yell Fire in a Crowded Office

Never fire someone out of the blue. Always issue a warning. Explain what the problem is, and give the employee a specified period of time to improve job performance. The average at most companies is 30 days. Make sure you are as clear with employees as possible that if they do not improve whatever it is they are doing (or not doing), then you will have to let them go. After the person leaves your office, you jot down a memo and save it to file so you can refer to it at a later day if necessary. An employee is less likely to get angry if he is fired when he is told well in advance what the consequences of his actions could be. This should be in writing and signed by the employee, so there is zero misunderstanding.

the control group after a six-month period (Brickman, Coates, and Janoff-Bulman 1978). Think about this for a moment. Whether we win a million dollars or become paralyzed, once the initial adjustment period ends, our overall emotional well-being and satisfaction with life does not fluctuate.

Whether it's a new assistant, a larger expense account, or the ability to work from home once a month, wait just long enough for him to settle into his new reality, and then the good news will more significantly shift his attitude.

## Strategy 8: Perspective Realignment

How we see our world and feel about the changes we experience is filtered through the lens of perspective, regardless of the actual objective reality. Let's take an example: If you have ever known someone who has had a traffic accident, you noticed that his subsequent driving changes. For example, if he tried to move into the left lane and did not see the oncoming car that subsequently hit him, he might become more thorough, even overly thorough, when shifting lanes in the same way again. Or perhaps someone who has been recently rear-ended might glance up at the rearview mirror more often, out of an exaggerated fear of a repeat scenario.

Even reading the newspaper can change how we see our world and ourselves. For instance, after hearing about a major plane crash, people tend to overestimate their personal vulnerability to the risk of flying. The reason is this: The crash is most available in memory. The odds have not changed, yet our perceptions have changed. Subsequently, our thoughts, attitudes, and behavior follow. We literally become more afraid, even though statistically and realistically speaking, nothing has changed.

You can radically alter how a person perceives information by first slightly shifting his perspective. In doing so, you create an internal hypersensitivity. Once he learns about the unemployment rate, company-wide cutbacks, or that several people were fired, he now weighs these factors more heavily. Therefore, from his perspective, he is lucky to only have to, say, relocate or assume more duties, considering how widespread the unfortunate circumstances have been for so many others.

When a person says, "It's not fair," what he really means is that in *comparison* with what other people got or have, he seems to have wound up with a bad deal. What seems fair bends, depending, then, on the law of contrast and comparison. For example, under what circumstances would an employee be upset that he received an 18-carat-gold Rolex watch? If his coworker got the same watch with a diamond bezel. Therefore, reminding him of those who were laid off or shifted to even less desirable working conditions will enable him to better appreciate his own fortunes.

See also:

- Chapter 1: *The Psychological Strategy to Gain Ironclad Loyalty: Never Lose an Employee, Customer, Client, or Employee Again*
- Chapter 4: *Turbo-Boost Morale and Keep Your Employees Productive, Motivated, and Happy . . . All without Spending a Dime*
- Chapter 13: *The Five Psychological Keys to Accomplish Any Goal*

# Conclusion

Dear Reader:

We have learned how to produce dramatic results with the application of some basic psychology. With these techniques you will be able to more effectively and successfully deal with a wide variety of some of the most common yet challenging business challenges.

We should strive to keep in mind that good judgment is required when applying your strategies; and just because you can get the upper hand in a situation, it does not always mean, that it is going to be the good and proper thing to do.

Sometimes the most responsible use of power comes by exercising restraint, and choosing to do what is right, even when this path lays contradictory to our own interests.

I hope that your personal and business life will be, in some way, improved as a result of this book and I welcome your thoughts, insights, and suggestions.

Feel free to write to me at: DJLMedia@aol.com

All the best,
David J. Lieberman

# Bibliography

Amabile, T. M. (1993). "Motivational synergy: Towards new conceptions of intrinsic and extrinsic motivation in the workplace." Human Resource Management Review 3: 185–201.

Ariely, Dan. *Predictably Irrational*. New York: HarperCollins, 2008.

Bailenson, Jeremy, Nick Yee, Kayur Patel, and Andrew C. Beall. "Detecting Digital Chameleons." *Computers in Human Behavior* 24 (January 2008).

Bandler, Richard, and John Grinder. *The Structure of Magic*. Palo Alto, CA: Science and Behavior Books, 1975.

Batiste, Linda Carter. "Accommodation and Compliance Series: Employees with Drug Addiction." Job Accommodation Network. http://www.jan.wvu.edu/media/drugadd.html.

Baxter, L. R., et al. "Caudate Glucose Metabolic Rate Changes with Both Drug and Behavioral Therapy for Obsessive-Compulsive Disorder." *Archives of General Psychiatry* 49 (1992): 681–689.

Brickman, P., D. F. Coates, and R. Janoff-Bulman. (1978). "Lottery Winners and Accident Victims: Is Happiness Relative?" *Journal of Social and Personality Psychology* 36 (1978): 917–927.

Carnegie, Dale. (1936) How to Win Friends and Influence People. Simon & Schuster.

Cialdini, R. B., and D. A. Schroeder. "Increasing Compliance by Legitimizing Paltry Contributions: When Even a Penny Helps." *Journal of Personality and Social Psychology* 34 (1976): 599–604.

Cialdini, R. B., J. E. Vincent, S. K. Lewis, J. Catalan, D. Wheeler, and B. L. Darby. "Reciprocal Concessions Procedure for Inducing Compliance: The Door-in-the-Face Technique." *Journal of Personality and Social Psychology* 31 (1975): 206–215.

Cialdini, Robert B. *Influence: The Psychology of Persuasion.* New York: HarperCollins, 1998.

Diener, E., S. C. Fraser, A. L. Beaman, and R. T. Kelem. "Effects of Deindividuation Variables on Stealing among Halloween Trick-or-Treaters." *Journal of Personality and Social Psychology* 33 (1976): 178–183.

Dolnik, L., et al. "Stealing Thunder as a Courtroom Tactic Revisited: Processes and Boundaries." *Law and Human Behavior* 27 (2003): 267–287.

Flor, H. "Spouses and Chronic Pain." Lecture, annual meeting of the Society of Neuroscience, Orlando, FL, November 3, 2002.

Fournies, Ferdinand F. *Why Employees Won't Do What You Tell Them to and What to Do about It.* New York: McGraw-Hill, 1999.

Freedman, J. L., and S. C. Fraser. "Compliance without Pressure: The Foot-in-the-Door Technique." *Journal of Personality and Social Psychology* 4 (1966): 195–202.

Gallup. "Can Employees Be Friends with the Boss?" *Gallup Management Journal.* http://gmj.gallup.com/content/23893/Can-Employees-Friends-Boss.aspx.

Garner, Randy. "What's in a Name? Persuasion Perhaps." *Journal of Consumer Psychology* 7 (2005).

Garner, Randy. "Post-It Note Persuasion: A Sticky Influence." *Journal of Consumer Psychology* 7 (2005): 627–639.

Goleman, Daniel, Richard Boyatzis, and Annie McKee. *Primal Leadership: Realizing the Power of Emotional Intelligence.* Boston: Harvard Business School Press, 2002.

Gordon, R. A. "Impact of Ingratiation on Judgments and Evaluations: A Meta-Analytical Investigation." *Journal of Personality and Social Psychology* 71 (1996): 51–70.

Gottman, John. *Why Marriages Succeed or Fail: And How You Can Make Yours Last.* New York: Simon & Schuster, 1995.

Greenberg, J. "Who Stole the Money, and When? Individual and Situational Determinants of Employee Theft." *Organizational Behavior and Human Decision Processes.* 89 (2002): 985–1003.

Guadagno, R. E., and R. B. Cialdini. "Online Persuasion: An Examination of Gender Differences in Computer Mediated

Interpersonal Influence." *Group Dynamics: Theory, Research and Practice* 6 (2002): 38–51.

Haney, C., C. Banks, and P. Zimbardo. "Interpersonal Dynamics of Simulated Prison." *International Journal of Criminology and Penology* 1 (1973): 69–97.

Herman, Roger E. *Facilitative Leadership*. San Francisco: Berrett Koehler, 2000.

Holmes, T., and R. Rahe. "Social Readjustment Rating Scale." *Journal of Psychosomatic Research* 11 (1967): 214.

Iyengar, S. S., and M. R. Lepper. "When Choice Is Demotivating: Can One Desire Too Much of a Good Thing?" *Journal of Personality and Social Psychology* 79 (2000): 995–1006.

Kahneman, D., and A. Tversky. "Prospect Theory: An Analysis of Decision under Risk." *Econometrica* 47 (1979): 263–291.

Kohn, Alfie. *Punished by Rewards: The Trouble with Gold Stars, Incentive Plans, A's, Praise, and Other Bribes*. Boston: Houghton Mifflin, 1999.

KPMG. "Profiles of a Fraudster Survey 2007." http://www.in.kpmg. com/pdf/KPMG_Profile_of_a_%20Fraudster_Survey%202007_ Forensic.pdf.

Kresevich, Millie. "Using Culture to Cure Theft, Loss Prevention & Investigations." *Entrepreneur*, February 2007.

Krumhuber, E., A. Manstead, and A. Kappas. "Temporal Aspects of Facial Displays in Person and Expression Perception: The Effects of Smile Dynamics, Head-Tilt, and Gender." *Journal of Nonverbal Behavior* 31 (2007): 39–56.

Leventhal, H., R. Singer, and S. Jones. "The Effects of Fear and Specificity of Recommendation upon Attitudes and Behavior." *Journal of Personality and Social Psychology* 2 (1965).

Lieberman, David J. *Never Be Lied to Again*. New York: St. Martins, 1998.

Lieberman, David J. *Get Anyone to Do Anything*. New York: St. Martins, 2001.

Lieberman, David J. *Make Peace with Anyone*. New York: St. Martins, 2002.

Lieberman, David J. *You Can Read Anyone*. Lakewood, NJ: Viter Press, 2007.

Lipsitz, A., K. Kallmeyer, M. Ferguson, and A. Abas (1989). Counting on blood donors: Increasing the impact of reminder calls. *Journal of Applied Social Pscyhology*, 19.

Livingstone, S., and P. Lunt. "Savers and Borrowers: Strategies of Personal Financial Management." *Human Relations* 46 (1993): 963–985.

Loehr, Jim, and Tony Schwartz. *The Power of Full Engagement.* New York: Free Press, 2004.

Mas, Alexandre, and Enrico Moretti. "Peers at Work," NBER Working Paper 12508. Cambridge, MA: National Bureau of Economic Research, September, 2006. http://www.nber.org/papers/w12508.

Mayo, Elton. Papers, 1909–1960. Baker Library, Harvard Business School, Boston.

McClurg, L. A., and D. S. Butler. "Workplace Theft: A Proposed Model and Research Agenda." *Southern Business Review* 31 (2006): 25–34.

Medvec, V. H., S. F. Madey, and T. Gilovich. "When Less Is More: Counterfactual Thinking and Satisfaction among Olympic Medalists." *Journal of Personality and Social Psychology* 69 (1995): 603–610.

Meltzoff, A. N., and J. Decety. "What Imitation Tells Us about Social Cognition: A Rapprochement between Developmental Psychology and Cognitive Neuroscience." *Philosophical Transactions of the Royal Society* 358 (2003): 491–500.

Moeland, R. L., and R. B. Zajonc. "Exposure Effects in Perception: Familiarity, Similarity, and Attraction." *Journal of Experimental Social Psychology* 41 (1982).

Moody's Investor Services. http://Moodys.com.

Moormon, Robert H., Gerald L. Blakeky, and Brian P. Niehoff. "Does Perceived Organizational Support Mediate the Relationship between Procedural Justice and Organizational Citizenship Behavior?" *Academy of Management Journal* 41 (1998).

Nelson, Bob. *The Ten Ironies of Motivation.* San Diego, CA: Nelson Motivation, 2002.

Parkinson, C. *Parkinson's Law: The Pursuit of Progress.* London: John Murray, 1958.

Pfau, Bruce, and Ira Kay. *The Human Capital Edge: 21 People Management Practices Your Company Must Implement (or Avoid) to Maximize Shareholder Value*. New York: McGraw-Hill, 2001.

Pfeffer, J., C. T. Fong, R. B. Cialdini, and R. R. Portnoy. "Overcoming the Self-Promotion Dilemma: Interpersonal Attraction and Extra Help as a Consequence of Who Sings One's Praises." *Personality and Social Psychology Bulletin* 32 (2006): 1362–1374.

Rath, Tom. *Vital Friends: People You Can't Afford to Live Without*. New York: Gallup Press, 2006.

Ramsey, R. D., 2005, Interpersonal conflicts, SuperVision, Vol. 66, Iss. 4, pp 14–17, National Research Bureau, Burlington.

Rein, Irving, Philip Kotler, and Martin Stoller. *High Visibility*. New York: McGraw-Hill, 2005.

Rodin, J. "Aging and Health. Effects of the Sense of Control." *Behavioral Brain Res.* Vol. 4, pp. 36–42 (1994).

Santos, M., C. Leve, and A. R. Pratkanis. "Hey Buddy, Can You Spare 17 Cents? Mindfulness and Persuasion." Paper presented at the annual meeting of the American Psychological Association, San Francisco, August 1991.

Sarbanes-Oxley Act of 2002. U.S. Securities and Exchange Commission. http://www.sec.gov/about/laws/soa2002.pdf.

Schmuck, P., et al. "Intrinsic and Extrinsic Goals: Their Structure and Relationship to Wellbeing in German and US College Students." *Social Indicators Research* 50 (2000).

Schweitzer, Maurice E., John C. Hershey, and Eric Bradlow. "Promises and Lies: Restoring Violated Trust." Social Science Research Network (March 2004). http://ssrn.com/abstract=524782.

Shermer, Michael. "The Belief Module." *Skeptic* 5 (1997): 78.

Sklar, Leonard. *The Check Is Not in the Mail: How to Get Paid More in Full, on Time, at Less Cost and without Losing Valued Customers*. San Mateo, CA: Baroque, 1990.

Slovic, Paul. "If I Look at the Mass I Will Never Act: Psychic Numbing and Genocide." *Judgment and Decision Making* 2 (2007): 1–17.

Taylor, T., & Booth-Butterfield, S. (1993). Getting a foot in the door with drinking and driving: A field study of healthy influence. *Communication Research Reports*, 10, 95–101.

Thomas, Kenneth W. *Intrinsic Motivation at Work*. San Francisco: Berrett Koehler, 2000.

Tiedens, L., C. Peterson, and F. Lee. "Mea Culpa: Predicting Stock Prices from Organizational Attributions." *Personality and Social Psychology Bulletin* (forthcoming).

Thaler, R. H. & Sunstein, C. R. Nudge: Improving Decisions About Health, Wealth, and Happiness (Yale University Press, 2008).

Tversky, A., and D. Kahmneman. "The Framing of Decisions and the Psychology of Choice." *Science* 211 (1981): 453.

Vedantam, Shankar. "Persistence of Myths Could Alter Public Policy Approach." *Washington Post*, September 4, 2007, A03.

Weaver, K., S. M. Garcia, N. Schwarz, and D. T. Miller. "Inferring the Popularity of an Opinion from Its Familiarity: A Repetitive Voice Can Sound Like a Chorus." *Journal of Personality and Social Psychology* 92 (2007): 821–833.

Workplace Bullying Institute. "2007 WBI-Zogby U.S. Workplace Survey." http://bullyinginstitute.org.

Zimbardo, P. G. "The Human Choice: Individuation, Reason, and Order versus Deindividuation, Impulse, and Chaos." In W. J. Arnold and D. Levine (eds.), *1969 Nebraska Symposium on Motivation* (pp. 237–307). Lincoln: University of Nebraska Press, 1970.

# About the Author

**David Lieberman, PhD,** is an award-winning author and internationally recognized leader in the field of human behavior and interpersonal relationships. Techniques based on his seven books, which have been translated into 21 languages and include two *New York Times* best sellers, are used by the FBI, the Department of the Navy, *Fortune* 500 companies, governments, corporations, and mental health professionals in more than 25 countries. He has appeared as a guest expert on hundreds of programs such as *The Today Show, Fox News, The Montel Williams Show, The O'Reilly Factor,* and *The View,* and his work has been featured in publications around the world.

# Index

**A**
Abas, A., 52
Adams, Douglas, 103
Air France, 15–16
Amabile, Theresa, 35
Ariely, Dan, 43, 72
Asch experiment, 140–141

**B**
Bailenson, Jeremy, 152, 153
Beall, Andrew C., 152
Beaman, A. L., 21
Blakely, Gerald L., 39
Bluffing:
    confidence and level of
        interest, 119
    confidence vs. self-esteem,
        112–113
    direction of attention,
        117–119
    and eye contact, 115
    and overcompensation,
        114–116
    perception management,
        113–117
    and physical factors, 117

and superfluous gestures,
    116–117
Boorstin, Daniel J., 11
Booth-Butterfield, S., 43
Bradlow, Eric, 14
Brickman, P., 181
Bridgestone, 15–16
Bullying in the workplace:
    handling passive-aggressive
        behavior, 137–138
    overview, 130–131
    refocusing the dialogue,
        135–137
    refusing ownership, 133
    rejecting the premise,
        131–133
    rising above unwanted
        advice, 134–135
    statistics of, 130
Butler, D. S., 39

**C**
Carnegie, Dale, 75, 153
Centers for Disease Control
        and Prevention (CDC),
        16–17

**W**
Wall Street Journal's
    CareerJournal.
    com, 28
Weaver, Kimberlee, 141
Western Electric
    Company, 30
*Why Employees Don't Do
    What They're Supposed
    to Do* (Fournies), 31

Workplace Bullying
    Institute, 130
Wrigley, William Jr., 167

**Y**
Yee, Nick, 152
*You Can Read Anyone*
    (Lieberman), 113

**Z**
Zogby International, 130